Education and Children
with Special Needs

Education and Children with Special Needs

From Segregation to Inclusion

Editors

Seamus Hegarty
Mithu Alur

Sage Publications
New Delhi ▢ Thousand Oaks ▢ London

First published in 2002 by

Sage Publications India Pvt Ltd
M 32 Market, Greater Kailash I
New Delhi 110 048

Sage Publications Inc
2455 Teller Road
Thousand Oaks, California 91320

Sage Publications Ltd
6 Bonhill Street
London EC2A 4PU

Published by Tejeshwar Singh for Sage Publications India Pvt Ltd, typeset by Asian Telelinks in 10pt Humanst521 BT and printed at Chaman Enterprises, Delhi.

Library of Congress Cataloging-in-Publication Data

Education and children with special needs: from segregation to inclusion/ editors, Seamus Hegarty, Mithu Alur.
    p. cm.
Includes bibliographical references and index.
    1. Children with disabilities—Education—India. 2. Children with disabilities—Education—Cross-cultural studies. 3. Inclusive education—India. 4. Inclusive education—Cross-cultural studies. I. Hegarty, Seamus. II. Alur, Mithu, 1943–
LC4037.14 E38   371.9'0954—dc21   2002   2002017312

ISBN: 0–7619–9584–6 (US–Hb)   81–7829–096–0 (India–Hb)
        0–7619–9585–4 (US–Pb)   81–7829–097–9 (India–Pb)

Sage Production Team: Shweta Vachani, Rajib Chatterjee and Santosh Rawat

Dedication

This book is dedicated to the millions of children in India who have remained acutely marginalised and out of existing services because they are supposed to be disabled. It is hoped by the authors that a day will come when, instead of the segregation and separation from which they suffer today, their needs are understood and they are accepted and included into the regular educational system.

Contents

List of Abbreviations

AWW	Anganwadi worker
AIIMS	All India Institute of Medical Sciences
CBR	Community Based Rehabilitation
CDF	Canadian Development Fund
CIDA	Canadian International Development Agency
CSIE	Centre for Studies in Inclusive Education
DSERT	Department of State Education, Research and Training
DIET	District Institute of Education Training
DPEP	District Primary Education Programme
DPI	Disabled People International
EFA	Education for All
EPID	Educational Programmes Implementation
GOI	Government of India
HRD	Ministry of Human Resource Development
ICDS	Integrated Child Development Scheme
IEDC	Integrated Education for Disabled Children
IEP	Individual Educational Programme
IED	Integrated Education Development
IGNOU	Indira Gandhi National Open University
MARP	Multi-site Action Research Project
MCT	Multi Category Training
MOW	Ministry of Welfare
MSU	Maharaja Sayajirao University
NAD	Norwegian Association for the Disabled
NCCP	National Centre for Cerebral Palsy

NCERT	National Council of Educational Research and Training
NCTE	National Council for Teacher Education
NFE	Non Formal Education
NIE	National Institute of Education
NIED	National Institute of Educational Development
NIEPA	National Institute of Educational Planning and Administration
NIPCCD	National Institute for Public Co-operation and Child Development
NIVH	National Institute of Visually Handicapped
NPE	National Policy on Education
NRCI	National Resource Centre for Inclusion
NUT	National Union of Teachers
PIED	Project on Integrated Education for the Disabled
POA	The Programme of Action
RDIER	Royal Danish Institute of Educational Research
RDSED	Royal Danish School of Educational Studies
SEN	Special Education Need
SIA	Seva-in-Action
SSI	Spastic Society of India
TISS	Tata Institute of Social Sciences
UGC	University Grants Commission
UPE	Universal Primary Education
VIC	Visually Impaired Children
WCD	Women and Child Development (A GOI reference)

Preface and Acknowledgements

The test of our progress is not whether we add more to the abundance of those who have much; it is whether we provide enough for those who have too little.

(Roosevelt, 1937)

Children and young people with disabilities continue to be one of the most disadvantaged groups in all our societies. In addition to their manifest limitations they are subject to social discrimination, reduced work opportunities and—most damagingly of all—impoverished educational experiences. Roosevelt's stirring words and the call to arms which they implied are, if anything, more relevant today in relation to people with disabilities than they were in New Deal America of the 1930s.

Accepting there is a problem and knowing what to do about it are quite different things of course. One way of making progress is to look across countries, observe different cultural and organisational structures, and *in the light of this broader perspective* look at one's own situation with new eyes. It is not and must never be simply a matter of importing practice from elsewhere. What works in Birmingham or Kansas will not necessarily work in Delhi. What *can* be transported are the principles that underlie effective practice. How these principles are embodied in provision will vary from place to place, and intimate knowledge of local contexts is necessary for this to happen.

Learning from other countries' experiences has been particularly widespread in special education. In Europe and the northern countries generally, special education practice and thinking are very varied. It is commonly accepted, however, that children with disabilities and learning difficulties should be educated alongside their age peers and within the same curriculum frameworks to the greatest extent possible. This common understanding did not come from one place at one time. It emerged—unevenly—over a long period of time from the 1960s onward, from Scandinavian ideas on normalisation, Italian approaches to de-institutionalisation, the US concept of least restricted environment, and British thinking and practice focused around special educational needs.

If we accept as our goal a situation where all children and young people, whatever their level of disability, are fully part of their community and the community's institutions such as schooling, the key interest is how we can achieve that goal and what steps we must take to move along the line from rejecting or ignoring fellow citizens to creating the kind of communities where everybody's human rights are acknowledged to the fullest extent possible.

The actions to be taken can be examined at two levels: the level of the system, and the level of the school. There is a great deal of interaction between the two levels: decisions taken at system level affect what happens in the schools, and developments at school level can affect policies for the system as a whole. System-level considerations include legislation, administrative support, resourcing, professional development, support services and research. Action at school level encompasses classroom organisation and practice, resource utilisation, curriculum modification, parental involvement and so on.

The purpose of this timely book is to reflect on these principles and practices in the context of present-day India in the light of practice in other parts of the world. It draws on a dynamic series of conferences held across India where a diverse range of Indian and other experts examined the state of play with regard to inclusive education. If we are to rise to the challenge of providing enough for those who have too little, the issues raised here with clarity and passion must be addressed. A society which fails to provide for its most disadvantaged is thereby diminished. Progress is possible, however, as numerous Indian and other examples testify, and it is hoped that this book will play some small part in enhancing the educational opportunities—and the lives—of young Indians with disabilities.

I would like to acknowledge our appreciation to Sage Publications for their social concern in the education of children with disabilities, an area suffering centuries of neglect in India. The subject was eagerly discussed in a series of conferences held in Mumbai, Delhi and Jaipur. These conferences were sponsored by the Government of India's Ministry of Human Resource Development and were jointly presented by the ministry together with the NCERT and the Spastics Society of India, Mumbai to stimulate discourse on a subject which had not previously had any exposure to a public debate in India. The aim of the conferences was to alert the country to the need for change and update it about developments in other countries. The conferences examined the barriers in the way of equalisation of opportunities and the inclusion of children with disabilities into regular schools. It explored what was happening in the developed countries as well as in India and allowed a sharing of experiences and exchange of ideas. A main aim also was to learn from the experiences of others and help in building an environment and philosophy conducive to inclusion; to ensure that participants, which included government officials, policy makers, parents, professionals and disabled activists, have an opportunity for discourse and thus develop a new vision for the future with a view to changes in policy and practice. The idea was to help build different paradigms and support systems which would be culture-specific to India and would enable children with disabilities to be part of the ordinary system of education wherever possible.

The conferences were very well attended and the keen interest displayed in the proceedings was indicative of the concern for the issue of inclusion. The contributors of the conferences included leading exponents in the field of disability from all over India as well as from abroad. The international exponents included Mark Vaughan (UK), Karl Stukat (Sweden), Peter Gam Henriksen (Denmark), Rachel Golan and Margaret Yekutiel (Israel). The national experts were policy makers from both the government and key NGOs, such as the ex-education secretary P.R. Dasgupta, Abhimanyu Sinha, Champak Chaterjee, R.S. Pandey, Sudhesh Mukhopadyaya, Anupam Ahuja, Professor A.S. Sharma (Government of India), N.K. Jangira, Javed Abedi (Delhi), Varsha Hooja, Madhuri Pai, Vandana Garware (Mumbai), Reena Sen (Calcutta), Mita Nundy (Delhi), Uma Tulli (Delhi), Ruma Bannerjee (Bangalore), Poonam Natarajan, Usha Ramakrishnan (Chennai), S.S. Mani (Coimbatore), Anil Bordia, Pearl Kavoori, Deepak Kalra (Jaipur) and many other eminent people. The authors are grateful to all of them: their valuable and context-specific contributions have been documented in this book. This book is the first of its kind on this subject, exploring the complex ramifications of educating children with disabilities within existing educational systems.

Reference

Roosevelt, F.D. (1937) 'Second Inaugural Address'. Washington D.C.: Library of Congress.

Introduction

Mithu Alur

Inclusion of persons with disabilities, especially inclusive education, is a concept that is gaining ground all around the world. To be clear about the nomenclature being used here, let me explain what the terms integration and inclusion mean in the context of the education of children with disabilities. The term 'integration' means the placing of children with special educational needs in ordinary schools. The term 'inclusion' has a deeper connotation and does not only refer to children with disabilities, but includes all children who face some kind of barrier to learning. It has a larger philosophy in the acceptance of diversity and how we deal with different children and their needs in the regular school system, teaching all children to understand and accept differences.

Given that this is a subject which is relatively new all over the world and especially so in India, I have attempted in this chapter to give an overview of how the change from segregated education to integration and then inclusion has taken place and the various factors underpinning the development in two developed countries, US and the UK. Second, I have highlighted the areas of policy formulation and implementation that exist for educating disabled children in India—the sociological perspective, the ideological and cultural underpinnings in which policy can become embedded; the historical and philosophical issues within the educational framework, within which policies exist. Much of the data is based on a recently completed Ph.D. I was awarded from the Institute of Education, University of London which was about disability and policy in India. The chapter ends with a brief overview of what each contributor has described in areas of legislation, policy and practice both from India and from abroad, with some concluding observations.

The International Context: From Segregation to Integration—The History and Ideology

Historically, reviewing the evolution of integration in the developed countries, we find that the crucial importance of the language used to describe children with disabilities was recognised. In an effort to dispel the stigma associated with the negative labels of the past, the old language which labelled disabled people as 'lame', 'defective', 'crippled', 'less fortunate', 'mentally retarded', 'epileptic', 'spastic', 'deaf and mute', all of which focused on their imperfections, was abandoned and replaced by the new language whereby children with disabilities were described in broader, more general terms such as 'children with special educational needs'. The old language of disability, it was argued, implied a mistaken model seeing difficulties within the individual child and disregarding the numerous facets in the external environment which disabled the child. This approach was regarded as a medical approach and known as the medical model. Today the approach is a social one looking, instead, at all the barriers within the environment that can disable a person.

Another important evolution that took place was the recognition of early educational opportunities. A compelling body of knowledge is available which shows that early intervention has powerful benefits for the growing child as well as the disabled child and that the disabled child develops profound problems physically, behaviourally and educationally without it. Substantial studies indicate that children with disabilities in integrated groups participated twice as much in social interaction and displayed higher levels of play than did children in the segregated groups. Integrated classes offer more opportunities for children to acquire skills with their peer group than do self-contained special education classes.

In 1978, in Britain, the Warnock Committee Report, a landmark in the history of education in the UK, listed essential provisions for children under five, and included children with disabilities as one of its three top priorities. The reasons given were that early identification and detection of children 'at risk' prevented special needs developing later. Great emphasis was placed on the earliest possible intervention, suggesting that every effort should be made to absorb disabled children into nursery schools in the areas where they lived. The Education Act, 1981, which followed, reiterated that no disabled child should be sent to a special school 'who can satisfactorily be educated in an ordinary school'. The role of 'parents in partnership' was emphasised as critical. The Warnock Committee distinguished between three forms of integration: locational—that is, special units or classes in an ordinary school or a special school on the same site as an ordinary school; social—where locational integration exists, but social interchange also takes place between special and normal; and functional integration—which involves special children joining their normal peers in regular classes on a full- or part-time basis (Warnock, 1978).

In the United States in 1964, Lyndon Johnson, then President, launched a massive programme called Head Start. The Head Start Programme opened 3,300 programmes for thousands of children right across America, with the aim of improving children's intellectual, social and emotional development, and expanded at an unprecedented rate. What was again relevant was that Head Start, one of the largest preschool programmes in the world, admitted disabled children. Federal mandate required that at least 90 per cent of the children admitted were from families whose income fell below poverty line and at least 10 per cent of the enrolment had to consist of disabled children. In 1975, the Education for All Disabled Children Act in the US was enacted which mandated that free, equal and appropriate public education must be provided between three 3 and 21 years for children and young people with special needs.

The concept of normalisation in which disabled persons were to participate was referred to as placement in the 'least restrictive environment' (LRE). The process of normalisation in a least restricted environment would include provisions for disabled persons according to need and should be, to the maximum extent possible, provided in the types of community settings that are used by non-disabled persons.

Legislation had far-reaching effects in the United States. The Act required the US to provide educational and other services to disabled children between the ages of three and five, and in fact encouraged them to do so from birth. Over 100 universities in America got involved in innovative research and evaluation focused on the problems of disadvantaged and disabled children. The Americans With Disabilities Act (ADA), signed into law by President Bush on 26 July 1990, established a clear and comprehensive federal prohibition of discrimination against persons with disabilities in private sector employment and sought to ensure equal access for persons with disabilities to public accommodation, public services, transportation and telecommunications.

Two issues are of particular significance: legislation was enacted and priority was given to under-five disabled children, in areas of preschool and treatment from the age of two, making it the responsibility of the state to ensure suitable provision; and preschool intervention based on principles of compensatory education was used to reduce the likelihood of children in socially deprived homes from dropping out and failing at school, as a preventive strategy in the early years, and this included the disabled child as well. The changes in language and the broader definition of 'special educational needs' marked a change from 'within the child to an interactive view'. Detailed multi-disciplinary assessment and a 'continuum of needs' were recognised, and close co-operation between special and ordinary schools suggested. Writing about the historical evolution that took place, Cole (1989) recounts that initially it was voluntary effort which made good the deficiencies in provision that existed. The intervention of the government followed to create a national framework in which public and voluntary agencies acted in partnership to see that all children, whatever their disability, received a suitable education (Cole, 1989). As the trend towards normalisation of experiences for disabled children gained pace, people began to question the efficacy of special schools. Groups of disabled people and parent pressure groups spoke vociferously about the needs for normalisation and tolerance from society as a whole. 'From being a rallying cry for those with a vision for change in special education, it became the new orthodoxy' and special schools not integration initiatives had to justify their existence (Hodgson et al., 1984).

The years that followed saw the enactment of legislation in many countries—Sweden, Norway, Italy, United Kingdom, Canada, Denmark, France and Germany—seeking integration or mainstreaming of children with special needs. The subject of segregation versus integration generated many debates. Those against integration argued that the old categories despite their negative labels had created appropriate education for disabled children within properly resourced environments and with people who understood the children. This was not always available in the regular schools. Evans (1995), writing about integration in the OECD countries, argues that 'it can be concluded, albeit tentatively, that integration is cost-effective and also offers the possibility for a more flexible use of precious funds for the benefit of all students' (Evans, 1995: 217).

The Wider Policy Framework: From Segregation to Inclusion—Values and Ideology

The subject of integration brought about a sea change in attitudes, a shift in ideology. The growing importance of the 'rights issue' was strongly stressed by disabled activists. Global initiatives on equalisation of opportunity, education for all, which are mentioned later in the book, reinforced this. Integration happened due to the changes in the wider educational system that had evolved due to many factors. There was a sea change mainly because of a growth in the understanding of children with disability, resulting in a change in attitude towards children with disabilities and stressing the paramount importance of integrating them in appropriate environments, suited to their special needs. This was followed by various Acts of Parliament which were later strengthened by fiscal support ensuring implementation. Today the new approach recommends access to a common schooling for all children, with access to a curriculum appropriate for all pupils. The challenge has become to examine ways and means of including all pupils who are different or diverse in any way; to create a system that ensures equality of value and combines the principles of comprehensive schooling as well as integration; to establish a whole-school approach where all children regardless of their capabilities, backgrounds, interests or handicaps are admitted (Booth and Potts, 1983: 27); to have an education system which accepts the 'ownership of any kind of diversity' and the principle that the aim of education should be to include all children (Wedell, 1995: 1), a philosophy built on the belief that all people are equal and should be respected and valued, as an issue of basic human rights. Stress is laid on the development of equal opportunities for all.

Inclusion and exclusion are processes which go together. Inclusive education is about minimising exclusion and fostering participation for all students in the culture within a wider framework of support for all children in ordinary schools. Inclusion is an unending set of processes in which children and adults with disabilities have the opportunity to participate fully in *all* community activities. An inclusive school might be said to be one that includes and values equally all students from its surrounding communities or neighbourhood and minimising groupings on the basis of attainment, gender or disability. The debates over segregation and inclusion in an ordinary school are related to wider ideologies of equal opportunity. Success depends on a school offering programmes which involve members of the broader community in decision making. There is also enough evidence to suggest that if the mechanism of intervention or the implementation process is to be worked out it makes more economic sense to have children in integrated set ups compared to costly special schools (World Bank, 1978).

Although there has been a change of attitude towards inclusive education, backed by legislation, inclusion has not been completely successful or fully accomplished. Progress has been uneven. This is partly due to the difficulties in bringing about a systems change. There have been lacunae between what has been stated and what has been implemented. This is due to many reasons, not least of all administrative and financial constraints. The process of distinguishing the needs of each child who may face some barrier to learning is a very complicated process needing an individualised approach. Research indicates that attitudinal factors could be major barriers to integration. These could be attitudes of teachers, peer group and parents themselves. Other factors are a lack of effective preparation of teachers, the limitations and constraints of many ordinary schools imposed by the national curriculum, the daunting challenge in differentiating the needs of each child.

The Indian Context: The Wider Framework— Some Fundamental Issues

The Social Structure

All this has been possible, in the developed countries, because of an ideological commitment to the philosophy of equal opportunity, and the fact that societal change at all levels is critical in placing disabled children and their families as part of the larger inclusive community. Together with an ideological commitment we find that there has been financial allocation where operational mechanisms have been worked out. These are issues which currently in India are matters of fundamental concern that need to be addressed if positive inclusion is to happen.

However, the practice of inclusion has its niche within an existing social system and a wider framework. In India the fundamental questions relating to gender issues, disability and poverty confront us when prioritising services. The social structure in India is within a highly stratified hierarchical set up. Indian society is submerged in concerns of class, caste, gender and religion, which is highly detrimental to social change.

Programmes of poverty alleviation, caste and gender issues, and rural upliftment take a higher priority, putting the disabled last on the list of development activity. The disabled are very much a part of these areas, but, mainly due to political weakness, they remain a neglected segment, kept out of the political and social framework of social policy. Social integration, which is meant to be an integral part of a society, is a far cry for Indian disabled people. India's policies are similar in some ways to what was happening in Britain during the pre-Warnock years, in the mid-1960s. Children with disabilities still remain enshrined in the ideologies of segregation, labelled and categorised according to the medical definition of their disability. This labelling is disabling. Labelling human beings dehumanises them. Their self worth gets devalued. It reduces them to objects of pity, sympathy or even of patronage. Underpinning the marginalisation that has taken place in India are stereotypical cultural and social ideologies dominating the minds of people.

The Social Construct of Disability

Disability and its conceptualisation are cultural and social constructs. Cross-cultural literature on disability suggests that a broader view of society is needed to understand the cultural underpinnings and value systems that dominate. It is now generally accepted that societal barriers place impediments in the way of persons with disabilities, preventing them from achieving their optimal levels. In the Indian situation, ignorance about disability is widespread. According to my research, there is a deep-seated prejudice about disability which needs addressing. Negative attitudes dominate, and disability is thought of as taboo and a stigma. This is all-pervasive and has affected the status in which disabled children are regarded and the way they are separated from the rest of their peer group. Disabled children, because of their lower worth, are denied the rights existing for the 'normal'. Disability is viewed as a personal tragedy, an individual problem concerning not the state but individual families.

Social exclusion takes place when human beings are stigmatised and put into narrow pathologised boundaries. The disabled tend to be losers in a situation which is divided up between those who are able or normal and those who are unable and disabled and considered abnormal. A person can overcome a disability but cannot overcome the entrenched negative beliefs.

We find that since Independence, the disabled have been classified with other vulnerable and weaker sections of the population, such as women and children, scheduled castes and scheduled tribes, but excluded from the services planned for other children. Government policies serving children in the poorer areas of the country do not include children with disabilities. This oppression in the form of a mandate from the top takes the form of institutionalised discrimination, resulting in social and educational exclusion from the mainstream.

The Educational System: Universal Education— A Dream Unrealised

Policy issues are part of a wider discourse. One of the most conspicuous failures of the Indian educational system has been the failure to achieve universal education. This is also one of the factors for the marginalisation that has taken place. This failure in achieving education for all goes back a number of years.

During the British period, primary and mass education did not receive any serious attention; only higher education was found to be important. The tilt towards higher education resulted in the neglect of primary education and, while India has been trying to remedy this, universal education has still not been achieved. The general feeling among the educational analysts is that India inherited 'a top-heavy, bottom weak, elitist unproductive, and irrelevant educational system from the British' (Naik, 1975: 13). Again, writers argue that although colonial policies of the past were responsible for some aspects of the current failures in education, India has to take the major share of the blame for its state policies in the post-Independence period (Aggarwal, 1992; Naik, 1975, 1980; Tilak, 1990).

It was only in 1953, at a national policy level, with the creation of the Central Social Welfare Board that the government started playing a role on a broader scale. Between 1960 and 1975, several national committees were appointed by the government to look into child welfare activities and these recommended that a comprehensive national policy was needed to take an integrated view of the needs of children in socially disadvantaged areas (Sood, 1987; Verma, 1994). In 1974, the National Policy for Children declared 'children as a supremely important asset of the nation whose nurture and solicitude are the responsibility of the nation', and The National Children's Board came into existence (ibid.). It was with the Fifth Five Year Plan[1] (1974) that a major breakthrough was made for the provision of early childcare by the state for children in socially disadvantaged areas, with the launching of the Integrated Child Development Scheme (ICDS), the largest preschool programme in the world. A significant factor that may have kept disabled children out of the purview of services is that disabled children did not come up as an issue for discussion during the policy formulation stage (Alur, 1999).

Disability: Charity and Welfare not Education— A Conceptual Confusion

In 1960, the Ministry of Education, which had been responsible for the education of disabled children, was bifurcated and the Ministry of Social Welfare created.[2] The MOW was entrusted with the responsibility for the vulnerable and weaker sections of society, with rehabilitation as the main objective. The weaker sections included the scheduled castes and tribes, women and children, and the disabled, the argument being that the weaker sections of society needed welfare and rehabilitation. Children with disabilities were not a part of the programmes that were created for the other weaker segments. The priority for education was not spelt out.

The government has developed four national level institutes. However, the national institutes are not involved with education and delivery of services. They remain costly, monolithic structures, their brief being rehabilitation not education.

In 1968, reviewing the status of educational developments for disabled children, Sargent reiterated that 'few people in these days would deny that provisions for those children who are physically or mentally handicapped should form an essential part of any national system of education' (Sargent, 1968: 109).

However, the matter was never taken up. To this day the issue remains undefined indicating a lack of policy commitment. Today, the government

---

[1] The five year plans were the mechanisms by which Government of India structured the economic development of India.

[2] Now known as the Ministry of Social Justice and Empowerment.

relies on voluntary organisations to set up basic facilities for education and treatment. The government's conceptualisation of the problem remains ingrained with the belief that the education and management of disabled children need voluntary action. Special schools exist for the blind, deaf, cerebral palsied, mentally handicapped and slow learners, run by NGOs. Except for a few training centres which have attached service facilities, and a few demonstration and research programmes for the development of service models, the government does not play a major role in providing services. The states have also lagged behind in opening new schools, vocational centres and rehabilitative institutions for the disabled.

Voluntary organisations can only serve on a micro level. The state's reliance on the voluntary sector has produced piecemeal services. The geographical logistics of the subcontinent and the expenditure incurred in travelling are barriers to frequent contact between the NGO groups, keeping them a fragmented and divided group. There is also no cross-disability movement. A Government of India survey indicates that 98 per cent of disabled people in the urban areas and 98 per cent in the rural areas are not being covered by any service at all.

India is amongst the few developing countries where the state relies heavily on the voluntary sector for providing basic services for the disabled on a micro level, resulting in patchy services and covering only a miniscule proportion of those in need.

This remains the policy for educating one of the most vulnerable and weakest groups of society—cultural injustice which has become historically entrenched.

The Conflict of Resources

The government spends 70 per cent of its planned expenditure on the four national institutes and factories it has set up for aids and appliances and only 30 per cent on the voluntary sector. A major factor for the evolution that has taken place in the West has been the availability of resources. In most countries, funding constraints for disabled children are a major issue. In India too there is undoubtedly a conflict of resources, the conflict being that resources should first be allocated for normal children, millions of whom are out of school. It has been written that the implementation of policy for facilitating integration is often reduced to a conflict over resources. However, this moves the discourse away from the need for an ideological commitment to inclusion and the rights of all children to education, most of all those who are vulnerable and at high risk of developing secondary deformities as children with disabilities.

There is first of all a need for the government to find the resources to initiate the shift in educational thinking. Policy without funding is no policy at all.

Conceptual Weakness

Tracking Indian social policy, one sees acknowledgement of the needs of children with handicap right from 1944 and the broad philosophical affirmative statements on paper to meet these educational needs within the regular school system. But due to a lack of conceptualisation, contradictory policies prevail, creating a lack of cohesion. Training institutions in the rehabilitation sector are few. Due to the limited number of training institutions, there is a shortage of trained personnel.

Confusion in conceptualising the needs of the normal child did not help in developing the issue. Instead of one agency dealing with the child and its multifaceted but diverse needs, the child has been 'dissected' into separate segments and its various needs distributed among separate ministries. Thus, we find the child in the workforce in the Ministry of Labour, the child in impoverished circumstances in Ministry of Education, child with a disability in the Ministry of Welfare. The framework within which the disability group seems buried is a framework of rehabilitation and care, not education.

The implementation procedures of the two ministries of HRD and Welfare have a dualism of purpose, causing ambiguity in the field. The government's assistance, in the way of grants-in-aid to voluntary organisations, has become officially accepted state policy. The continued reliance of the government on the NGO sector absolves it of its responsibilities towards the disabled as citizens with their own rights.

The Persons with Disability Act (PDA) 1995

What is significant, however, is that a new direction is noticeable. Global initiatives mentioned earlier have influenced India. A new legislation was enacted in 1994 known as The Persons with Disability Act which states that disabled children should, as far as possible, be educated in integrated settings.

This proposed Act was introduced in pursuance of India being a signatory to ESCAP, which had adopted a proclamation on the full participation and equality of people with disabilities in the Asian and Pacific Region.

The PDA is a landmark legislation in the disability movement in the country. It presents a vision for people with disabilities, people who have for centuries been victims of prejudice, neglect, ostracism, treated as lesser beings and consigned to the bottom heap of humanity. However, does the Act provide hope?

The intent of the proposed legislation is extremely laudatory as it is the first time that India recognises persons with disabilities as equal human beings. However, no rights have been conferred on them in the event of non-compliance by the state, nor is there any enforcement agency or fiscal support.

No adequate preparations have been made for implementation. Specialist services are being promised without the infrastructure to deliver them. No remedies have been provided for non-performance. On the contrary, Section 71 of the PDA protects the central and state governments and local authorities or any officer of the government from any suit, prosecution or other legal proceeding in respect of any act done in good faith or intended to be done under the Act. To this extent the proposed legislation remains a statement of pious intent, rather than a vibrant proactive instrument for the betterment of the millions of persons with disabilities and their families, who remain marginalised without any policy or substantive services.

To put the Act into practice, there is a need therefore to establish a goal-oriented task force for achieving affirmative action; to establish a regulatory framework that will periodically monitor achievements vis-à-vis predetermined targets in implementation of the act; and, most importantly, to establish an enforcement mechanism.

DPEP Issues

A programme called the District Primary Education Programme (DPEP) was launched in 1995 by the government, supported by the World Bank, with the aim of working out curricula, teacher training, etc., for early childhood care, including disabled children. The most significant change proposed is that the district primary schools in the state would be held responsible for all children, including disabled children. India was aiming to reach 'Education for All' status by the year 2000. The District Primary

Education Programme (DPEP) was started in 14 states of India. This is the first time that primary education has been delinked from the state. The primary objectives of the DPEP are to support Government of India's efforts towards universalisation of elementary education; address the issue of dropouts, out-of school children and early marriages by starting primary schools in every village; provide extensive teacher training; address gender issues and create programmes for the empowerment of women. Convergence of different government agencies and NGOs at various levels would be promoted actively; teachers would receive regular in-service training through the District Institute of Education and Training (DIET) and the State Council of Educational Research and Training (SCERT); case studies and statistics showing enrolment, retention, dropouts and gender-wise specifications would be compiled annually; alternate schooling would be promoted with a focus on flexible curriculum, informal evaluation criteria, flexible timings and other issues of adult illiterate persons; and, following world trends, integrated or inclusive education of children with mild to moderate disabilities would be promoted.

Achievements

Through the massive civil construction drive, over 200,000 new schools have been constructed. This has helped in increasing the number of school children and in spreading adult literacy. Women in villages are getting an opportunity to interact with each other. It is reported that through the mother-teacher associations, more girls are completing their basic education that before. Teachers have been exposed to modern education methods of teaching.

All teachers receive in-service training through the massive training drive promoted by individual states. In most states, IED is being promoted and strategies to achieve this are being developed.

Drawbacks

The non-formal education centres have not been effective. Objectives for the same are very unclear to most practitioners. Often, budgets are allocated for non-existent centres. High dropout problems still exist in tribal areas and in many of the districts with very low female literacy. Many schools continue to be one-teacher schools and the teacher finds multigrade teaching very difficult. Although school registrations have increased dramatically, learning achievement is still very low in many districts. Integration of the disabled is not been done and there is still very heavy reliance on special school systems.

With the establishment of the Persons with Disability Act and the DPEP programme, for the first time the government has made a firm statement on including children with disabilities into existing services. It is envisaged that through the infrastructure development the programme will be self sustaining and replicable to remaining states and districts not covered under the initial phase. The first phase of the programme was initiated in the educationally most backward districts of each state. In the second phase more districts were added.

However, this does not solve the overall lack of a cohesive government stand as far as the education of children with disabilities is concerned. Policy and practice during the post-Independence period seem to be similar to what was happening in pre-Independence India a 100 years ago where a policy of paternalism (of doling out grants in aid to charitable institutions) was the practice. Present government policy towards disabled children is equivocal and full of ambiguities, principally dependent on voluntary organisations to deliver services. India is amongst the few developing countries where the state relies heavily on the voluntary sector for providing basic services for the disabled. The non-government sector has pioneered valuable services, ensuring social integration into the community; however, with limited infrastructural services and funds, the voluntary sector has only served on a micro-level. This reliance contributes to a micro-level spread, covering only the tip of the iceberg. Rural areas still remain out of reach and, considering the fact that the majority of disabled people live in these areas, this very significant group of the Indian population remains neglected.

The government's ambivalence and silences, its non-decision making and its inaction in the face of this situation infringe basic human rights, indicating a lack of political will and ideological commitment. An inclusive policy examines all the barriers to learning. Until such time as implementation of policy takes place, India has not addressed the question of education of the disabled child in its policy statements and this is why it is excluded from its practice. The compartmentalisation, the invisible barriers, the non-decision making and the discrimination are symptomatic of the larger fragmentation that pervades the nation. The lack of a positive discriminatory statement including disabled children has led to neglect and silence which have been maintained through the years.

'Education for All' could remain an empty promise on the part of the Government of India if there are no plans to operationalise policy into practice. Today, due to the state's non-involvement, a staggering figure of over 90 per cent of India's disabled people remain without any provisions (GOI, 1994a).

It is important before one begins any journey to know about the pitfalls and barriers we will encounter. This gives us the insight we will need about the levels of intervention that are needed to overcome them. It is for this reason that I have tried to give in this introductory chapter an idea of the barriers we are facing. Some of these issues were brought up and discussed during the seminar. In the following sector I have briefly mentioned them and concluded with what emerged as a consensus.

The Issues Raised

National Perspectives

In Chapter 1, Mr P.R. Dasgupta, then Secretary, Ministry of Education—now known as Ministry of HRD—describes the post-Independence period. He goes into detail on the various schemes that exist under the Ministry of Human Resource Development. The National Policy on Education, 1986 brought the education of children with disabilities under the Equal Education Opportunity Provision. However, although policy states that wherever possible children with disability should be educated in general schools, this has not been fully achieved. There is no cohesive policy. There are two ministries which are responsible for the education of disabled children. The Ministry of Welfare is the nodal agency responsible for the welfare of handicapped children, which it does through the voluntary sector and special schools, and the Ministry of Education is responsible for integrated education through their Integrated Education for Disabled Children (IEDC).

In Chapter 2, I discuss my investigation of a particular policy of the Government of India, known as the Integrated Child Development Scheme (ICDS), which operates amongst the poorer sections of the population in India for preschool children in the age range of 0–6 years. The ICDS policy, although it states that it is for all children, does not in practice address the question of disabled children. Although it may have been the intention to include disabled children in the term 'all children', there is a gap between policy stated and policy enacted. Policies are not made in a vacuum. The chapter examines the sociocultural attitudes towards disability in the Indian subcontinent and explores the wider historical, political and ideological framework in which Indian social policy for the disabled exists. In any country, and particularly in a country like India, where there are severe resource constraints, issues tend to remain on the level of rhetoric without being translated into reality unless there is strong political support and an ideological commitment to see them through. The questions in this case are: Is there a strong and clear political commitment to put policy into action? What are the broader aspects of the disability discourse in India, since a major Government of India policy, such as the ICDS, continues not to include disabled children in their programmes, particularly in the late twentieth century?

N.K. Jangira, an expert on special education in the World Bank, confirms this situation in the country in Chapter 3. He discusses several issues why the education of children with special needs has never been included as a component in the plans for universal education. Financial allocations have been 'mostly nominal and ad hoc' compared with allocations proportionate to population, as has been the case with several other disadvantaged groups. According to him, 'plans and allocations should not be based on incidence but on prevalence of special educational needs, taking into consideration the backlog created due to decades of neglect'. Most of the teacher training activities are being conducted by the voluntary sector on the micro level. Due to the non-recognition of the issue of the need for educating children with disabilities, special educators do not get the compensation equivalent to their counterparts in regular schools. The disparity in the remuneration for teachers of normal children and disabled children is a key failure.

Special education has always had a mystique about it. It has invariably been construed as being highly technical needing a specialisation. Writers have suggested that this has been a key factor which has resulted in the medical model of labelling, categorising and segregating children with disabilities which is very much a part of the scene in India. In Chapter 4, Anupam Ahuja discusses this when she goes on to describe the Project on Integrated Education for the Disabled (PIED) carried out by the National Council of Educational Research and Training in collaboration with UNESCO. The rationale of the project was to encourage the development of mainstream classroom practices as part of the overall movement towards Education for All. It fitted in with the ideology of inclusive schooling intended to provide quality basic education to all children despite differences that may exist. However, due to the lack of financial support the project has not continued, again indicating the low priority given to this sector.

Rural Issues

The incidence of disability is pro rata to the population density, and therefore the incidence of disability in the rural and urban areas is according to the urban/rural population divide which is 30:70, 70 per cent of the disabled population being in rural India and the population density being less in the rural areas. Dr Mani, principal of the Ramakrishna Mission Teacher Training College, Coimbatore (Chapter 5) writes how 95 per cent of disabled children in the rural areas are scattered. The Government of India's efforts to pull in 'all the unreached children' has not been successful. He describes the need for teacher education and the need, as he describes it, is 'for single as well as multi-category teachers'.

In this context of pulling rural disabled children into the safety net, a pilot project on integrating disabled children within Maharashtra was planned. Madhuri Pai (Chapter 6) describes a DPEP programme functioning in rural Maharashtra. The chapter discusses the strategies used for the identification of children with special needs, their lifestyles and impediments for coming under the education umbrella. It also discusses the possibility of NGO support and strategies for manpower planning and development.

Integration in the rural areas is also discussed by Ruma Bannerjee of Seva-in-Action in Bangalore in Chapter 7. The community has been reached through grass-roots interaction with village-level committees. The practicalities of reaching the children through resource teaching after school hours and curriculum modification adapted to local needs are discussed in the chapter.

That integration is happening and successfully in different parts of the country comes through strongly in many chapters. Pearl Kavoori, a well known educationist from a mainstream background, discusses the ways she had approached the issue as principal of two major schools in Delhi and Jaipur in Chapter 8. The development of staff in accepting children with disabilities was critical, and a democratic way of functioning allowing confidence to develop helped to create a successful inclusive environment.

There is substantial evidence that strengthening remedial practices in an ordinary school helps disabled children as well as regular children. In Chapter 9, Usha Singh reiterates this as she describes several experiences of children with special needs who, with their determination and grit to succeed, showed that they could be successfully included in most activities. The crucial importance of in-service education, which is essential for mainstreaming, is emphasized by Usha Singh.

In Chapter 10, Father Augustine discusses the equalisation of opportunity for various sections of impoverished society that the Jesuit Schools have undertaken in Jaipur. Deepak Kalra (Chapter 11) talks about children who drop out of the system due to low motivation, neglect in the classes and poor teaching. Reena Sen investigates in Chapter 12 the difficulties of inclusion without clear policy directives, where students are dependent on the occasional sympathetic head teacher to get admission. Most educationists would agree that pedagogic issues need to be addressed and, as Reena Sen suggests, our general teacher training system needs to be equipped, methodologies for differentiation in curriculum planning has to be developed and pupil diversity recognised. Staff development and similar issues are also taken up as an integral part of the process of inclusion by Sudesh Mukhopadhyay (Chapter 13). She suggests the whole-school approach in bringing about change in schools and that teachers need to understand the learning style of their students with an individual approach to a learning situation. In the absence of appropriate preparation, she points out that there is a danger of harming children's education.

In Chapter 14, Amena Latif strongly states, from her own personal experience, that what one needs is a combination of the right environment and opportunity and a strong will to overcome for integration to be successful. In Chapter 15, Mark Vaughan, Director of the Centre for Inclusive Studies, brings up the fundamental issue of the matter of inclusion being now considered a matter of human rights and social justice. He describes the various International Declarations, the UN Standard Rules, the UN Convention of the Rights of the Child and the UNESCO Salamanca Statement which decrees that governments should give 'the highest policy and budgetary priority to improve education for all children'. He too endorses the whole-school approach if successful inclusive education is to be a reality.

Seamus Hegarty, Director of National Foundation for Educational Research, describes (Chapter 16) what has been achieved by developing countries today. All would agree when he writes that Education for All cannot be fully achieved unless special education moves on to a new phase of development. This entails action at system level and at school level. Action at system level must encompass: legislation, administration, the allocation of resources for educational provision, early childhood education, acknowledgement of parental rights, professional development, and research and development. The guiding concept at school level is the creation of one school for all. This requires action in respect of: academic organisation of the school, curriculum planning and pedagogy, inservice training, and parental involvement.

Karl-Gustav Stukat, eminent professor from Sweden, describes in Chapter 17 concepts of normalisation, integration and inclusion which have been official policy and widespread practice in Scandinavian countries since the late 1960s. Discussing mainly Swedish experience, he highlights the ideological considerations, the social forces and empirical research findings. He describes the need for internal consistency in the development of national guidelines. There is always a risk of harmful conflicts between overall educational goals and specific regulations, e.g., an inflexible grading system. Special and regular attention and training to teachers are critical. Peter Gam Henriksen (Chapter 18) writes about the Danish movement of non-segregation and describes comprehensive schools from which the movement of 'school for everyone' rose and thereafter all children with disabilities had a right to a meaningful education in the ordinary school system. He begins with examining the ideological premise behind the issue and describes the practicalities. Rachel Golan, in Chapter 19, writes about integration in Israel. In the process of implementing the Special Education Law (1988) the Department for Special Education worked out a national programme which demands fundamental recognition. Integration means organisational development of teamwork between professionals from the two sub-systems at different levels of our educational system.

Each time we work on the margin we redefine our society. Three models of integrative teamwork at class, school and community level gives example of the efforts made in Israel in order to give equal opportunities to exceptional children.

The Practice

The Bishopwood story of how a special school got desegregated in Britain is a good example of how people with a vision can change situations. Here, Mark Vaughan, in Chapter 15, describes the way 50 disabled children have been placed into ordinary schools. Today these children share the same lessons, join the same clubs and participate in the same activities as their peer group.

Success in modern life needs brain rather than brawn, and education is everywhere biased towards 'academic' achievement, with less than 10 per cent of the school hours given to physical education. Margaret Yekutiel from Israel writes in Chapter 20 about 'mind versus body bias and its effect in the cerebral palsied' and describes how this bias is especially marked in the education of children with disabilities who need maximum school hours to reach the academic achievements of their able-bodied peers. While other children exercise their bodies out of school through play or work, the disabled cannot. Indeed they are less likely to, the more they are aided by wheelchairs and helping hands. Lack of movement and play have wide repercussions on development, ranging from psychosocial disturbances to a life-threatening under-development of respiratory function, which is found to be 50–60 per cent less than that of normal children. Special methods and equipment, developed in Israel and other countries, to enable the child to move and play, promise improved health.

Malini Chib, in Chapter 21, writes about 'definitions' and what is politically correct. She looks at the real meaning of equalisation of opportunity and tries to get insight into her own special school background. Were there any disadvantages? Are disabled people totally accepted by society or are they still marginalised? In what way? *Is society willing to accept me as a thinking adult?*

The issues that were discussed were in the areas of policy, legislation, finance, the positive feature of the increase in the financial outlay for primary education in the Eighth Five Year Plan by which the budget for children with impairments increased by more than five times, ideological difficulties and the practicalities of inclusion, such as manpower training, curriculum adjustments, environmental adaptations. Educators at all levels are perplexed as to how to meet their responsibilities in the light of the Indian context: of overcrowded classrooms, lack of teachers being trained to handle and educate disabled children, the absence of infrastructure at university and college level for teacher education, and above all the lack of social and political pressures to enrol children with disabilities in regular classrooms. However, a strong consensus was reached and a resolution passed that the education of children with disabilities should be transferred to the Ministry of HRD, as it was in 1956 before the bifurcation of the Ministries of Welfare and Education was done. A resolution with more than 1,000 signatures was recorded and sent to the Ministry of HRD.

Concluding Observations: Ethics of the Question

Values reflect a society and its vision for its people. The reliance on NGOs makes the work isolated and piecemeal, moving away from the issue of provision, entitlements and right; from a macro level policy spread to segregation and marginalisation from mainstream society. The discourse is moved away from being a state responsibility absolving it of any accountability. A value system allotted to this group is one of paternalism, charity and welfare. This remains well ingrained within the social structure. The state is the source and the apparatus through which power is organised. Each society has its 'regimes of truth', the type of discourses it accepts and lets function as truth. These regimes are laid down, and can operate through social exclusion and marginalisation. These 'dividing practices' (Foucault, 1974: 49) have been used to legitimate actions. Today oppression and cultural injustice to the disability group have become entrenched. The voluntary sector taking on the government's responsibility have let the government off the hook. Many felt in the conferences that the NGO bandwagon was being misused by the government to save resources. The continuance of such a system suited the government's resource allocation for this group.

It would need major economic and social transformation to change attitudes to develop equality in education. This is specially so when the majority of families with disability are powerless in the grip of poverty and deprivation, their powerlessness leading to an unquestioning compliance with societal norms. To a certain degree, with positive discrimination towards children with disabilities, the required changes to include them into mainstream systems in the West have taken place. Emphasis now is on teaching and learning, on interacting with the environment, on understanding the needs of a wide range of diversity in moving away from labelling.

In India, even after 50 years one has achieved only 2 per cent coverage. A radical change in approach to the problems has to take place if we are to be considered a civil society in the comity of nations. The mere enactment of legislation without fiscal support for implementation only adds insult to injury and frustration.

In the West there have been years of segregated practice with special schools available for all types of disability. In India, the disabled child has not as many options, there being not enough special schools available.

Therefore, the rural child or the urban slum child does not have the option to go to a special school or to an integrated school. The most cost effective solution is to get service of some kind, and the local services, anganwadis, that already exist offer that.

The question remains a moral and ethical policy decision: Should India prioritise the needs of the normal child as the most urgent and postpone the decision to include the disabled child until such time as all normal children are in school? Should children be labelled on grounds of disability and kept out of the local nurseries especially when they are at a high risk of getting more disabled? What is the ethical and moral position India wishes to take in its explanation of the exclusion from basic welfare services? What kind of a society do we want? Is this cultural injustice in keeping with the spirit of the Constitution? The values of egalitarianism, social justice and moral ethics are values that need to have proper recognition in a society.

The need to legitimate services for *all* children and offering welfare benefits to all is critical. It is not just a single ministry but all government departments in fact; the nation should feel responsible for the exclusion taking place as it is against the spirit of the Constitution to allow education to suffer.

Inclusion is not just about children with disabilities. Citizenship has come into the forefront of the debate, making us understand what 'society' and 'civil society' stand for. In theory, the population is divided into two homogeneous groups—those who are within the national collectivity and those out of it. The 'underclasses' like women and people with disabilities are often lumped together. Disabled people are under-represented in all forms of public life. Disabled people's restricted access to decision making power in society has increased their political marginalisation and compounded many of the problems that they face (quoted in Chib, 2000). T.H. Marshall feels that citizenship refers to a basic kind of human equality for an individual, which is associated with the concept of full participation in society. *Without 'enabling' social conditions, political rights are vacuous.* Citizenship is based upon entitlements to resources, which guarantees a basic minimum level of comfort (Ramcharan and Borland, 1997: xi–xvi). Disability excludes people from being incorporated into the citizenship network, keeping them 'passive citizens'; disabled people have been effectively marginalised and excluded from the mainstream of social life, and this aspect of disabling society needs to be explored in the context of unequal power and social resources (Barnes, Mercer, Shakespeare, 1999). Rioux argues that disabled people need adjustments in social, economic and legal policies so that they can equally participate as citizens.

Civil society built on the dogmas of social justice and equal opportunity recognises the weak, the needy and the helpless. This conforms to the spirit of the Constitution and yet it is overlooked in the context of the disabled child. Educational practices are embedded in a larger framework of value system. To change it to a society where people value each other despite differences moves the discourse into the philosophy of egalitarianism and equality of opportunity for all.

It is sincerely hoped that this book generates discussion and discourse about children whose lives have so far remained invisible.

References

Aggarwal, J.C. (1992) *Education Policy in India—Retrospect and Prospect.* New Delhi: Shipra.

Alur, M. (1999) 'Invisible Children: A Study of Policy Exclusion'. Department of Policy Studies, Institute of Education, University of London.

Barnes, C., G. Mercer and **T. Shakespeare** (1999) *Exploring Disability.* London: Polity Press.

Booth, T. and **P. Potts** (1983) *Integrating Special Education.* Oxford: Blackwell.

Cole, T. (1989) *Apart or a Part? Integration and the Growth of British Special Education.* Milton Keynes: Open University Press.

Chib, M. (2000) Citizenship Linkage of Different Models of Disability. Unpublished paper, Department of Policy Studies, Institute of Education, University of London.

Evans, P. (1995) 'Integrating Students with Special Educational Needs into Mainstream Schools in OECD Countries', *Prospects*, 25(2): 201–18.

Foucault, M. (1976) *Mental Illness and Psychology.* Translated by Alan Sheridan. First edn. New York: Harper & Row.

Government of India (GOI) (1994a) 'Directory of NGOs Receiving Grants-in-Aid under Various Schemes of Ministry of Welfare.' New Delhi.

——— (1994b) 'Directory of Institutions Working for the Disabled in India'. CACU-DRC Scheme, Ministry of Welfare, New Delhi.

Hodgson, A., L. Clunies-Ross and **S. Hegarty** (1984) *Learning Together: Teaching Children with Special Educational Needs in the Ordinary School.* Windsor: NFER-NELSON.

Marshall, T.H. and **T. Bottomore** (1992) *Citizenship and Social Class.* Chicago: Pluto Press.

Naik, J.P. (1975) *Elementary Education in India: A Promise to Keep.* Reprint 1979. Bombay: Allied Publishers.

——— (1980) *Reflection on the Future Development of Education: An Assessment of Educational Reform in India and Lessons for the Future.* New Delhi: Asia Publishing House.

Ramcharan, P. and **J. Borland** (eds) (1997) 'Preface', in *Empowerment in Everyday Life, Learning Disability.* London: Jessica Kingsley.

Ramcharan, P. and **J. Borland** (eds) (1997) 'Preface', in *Empowerment in Everyday Life, Learning Disability*. London: Jessica Kingsley.

Rioux, M. and **M. Bach** (1994) *Disability is not Measles*. Canada: The Roeher Institute.

Sargent, J. (1968) *Society Schools, and Progress in India*. Oxford: Pergamon Press.

Sood, N. (1987) 'An Evaluation of Non Formal Preschool Education Component in Mangolpuri ICDS block', *NIPCCD Technical Bulletin*, I April.

Tilak, J. (1990) *The Political Economy of Education in India*. Buffalo, N.Y.: Comparative Education Center, State University of New York, Buffalo in Co-operation with the Department of Educational Studies, Curry School of Education, University of Virginia.

Verma, A. (1994) 'Early Childhood Care and Education in India', *International Journal of Early Years Education*, 2(2), Autumn.

Warnock Report (1978) 'Special Educational Needs: Report of the Committee of Enquiry into the Education of Handicapped Children and Young People'. HMSO, London.

Wedell, K. (1995) 'Making Inclusive Education Ordinary', *British Journal of Special Education*, 22(3). Reprinted by CSIE, Bristol BS6 6UE.

World Bank (1978) 'Ability in Pre-schoolers, Earnings and Home Environments'. Staff Working Paper No. 322. Washington D.C.: World Bank.

PART I

National Perspectives on Policy

Education for the Disabled

P.R. Dasgupta

India has witnessed a phenomenal expansion of educational opportunities in the post-Independence period. However, disabled children have not benefitted substantially from this growth in educational facilities. This is not to say that no work has been done in the field of disabled welfare. Considerable work has been done over the years both by the Government of India and the voluntary sector, with substantial increases in the allocation of funds over different Plan periods. The special education system has done pioneering work in the field of educating children with disabilities. It is, however, faced with several problems like limited coverage, lack of qualified teachers and a sheltered environment. It was to overcome some of these problems that the Ministry of Welfare launched the scheme for Integrated Education for Disabled Children (IEDC) in 1974. The implementation of this scheme was transferred to the Department of Education in 1982.

National Policy on Education, 1986 and Its Programme of Action

The National Policy on Education (NPE), 1986 brought the education of this group of children under the Equal Education Opportunity Provision. It envisaged:

Centrally Sponsored Scheme of Integrated Education for Disabled Children (IEDC)

(i) Accordingly, with the objective of providing educational opportunities for disabled children in common schools so as to facilitate their retention in the school system, this Department has been implementing a centrally sponsored scheme of Integrated Education for Disabled Children (IEDC) since 1982–83. The scope of the scheme includes preschool training for disabled children and counselling for parents. Under the scheme, 100 per cent financial assistance is provided, as per prescribed norms, for education of disabled children. This includes assistance towards:

- facilities for disabled children like books and stationery, uniform, transport allowance, readers' allowance for blind children, escorts' allowance for severely handicapped children and boarding and lodging charges for disabled children residing in hostels;
- setting up of resource rooms;
- resource teacher support in the ratio of 1:8 in respect of all disabled children except those with locomotor disabilities;
- survey for identification of disabled children and their assessment;
- purchase and production of instructional material;
- training and orientation of resource teachers and school administrators; and
- salary of an IEDC Cell at the state level to implement and monitor the programme.

(ii) The scheme is implemented through education departments of the state governments/union territories, autonomous organisations of statutory and voluntary organisations. Presently, 24 states/union territories are implementing the scheme and over 50,000 disabled children in 12,292 schools have been covered so far. A statement of grants released during the last five years is in Appendix I.

(iii) In addition, the Project on Integrated Education for the Disabled (PIED), with UNICEF assistance, was introduced in 1987 to strengthen the implementation of the IEDC scheme. This project was tried out in a selected block in ten states of Haryana, Madhya Pradesh, Maharashtra, Mizoram, Nagaland, Orissa, Rajasthan and Delhi. A block was taken as a project area and all the schools in the block were converted into integrated schools. The teachers under this project were given three types of training: a general one-week training (Level I) to all primary teachers in the project area; a more intensive training (Level II) to some teachers in each school to equip them to handle children with disability; and the multicategory training (Level III) of one year's duration provided by the colleges of NCERT. The teachers with Level III training were placed in the project block to function as resource teachers for a cluster of schools.

An external evaluation of this project in 1994 showed that not only the enrolment of disabled children increased considerably, but the retention rate among the disabled children was very high (95 per cent), much higher than that of normal children in the same blocks. It created a greater awareness about education of disabled children in general schools and even the teachers acknowledged that they were becoming better teachers by teaching disabled children. Over 6,000 disabled children have been covered in 1,382 schools under PIED.

(iv) The NCERT is providing technical and academic support to the programme. It has:

- developed print material such as identification checklists, an assessment schedule, a handbook for teachers, a functional assessment guide, and source books in modular form for various types of impairment like hearing and visually impaired;
- developed non-print material such as video films on IEDC and films on the special needs of parents;
- trained master trainers under the UP Education for All Project, in handling special needs of children in normal schools. A multi-site action research programme has also been launched in 23 DIETs and four regional institutes of education;
- under manpower development, NCERT organised a number of training programmes for teachers as well as IEDC workers for early identification of disabled children and Multi Category Training (MCT) programmes for resource teachers. Based on

the feedback received, the MCT programme is being reviewed to enable trainees to acquire working knowledge about the nature and need of children with visual, hearing, orthopaedic or mental disability. Orientation programmes for parents, community, administrators and teacher educators of DIETs have also been organised between 1988 and 1994; and

- undertaken a project entitled 'Examination Procedure for Children with Special Needs at the Elementary and Secondary Levels'. It is also working in the area of providing suitable classroom strategies and curriculum adaptations for these children.

(v) Due to financial constraints only an amount of Rs. 250 million was allocated for this scheme during the Eighth Plan period. With the given allocation, the coverage was expected to reach 50,000 disabled children by the end of the Eighth Plan. This has been achieved. The main problems in implementation of this scheme have been lack of financial resources, trained teachers and specialised aids, and inadequate priority by the state governments.

- education of children with locomotor disability and other mild disabilities in general schools;
- special schools for severely disabled children at district headquarters;
- reorientation of teacher training programmes by including a compulsory special education component in pre-service training of general teachers;
- provision of vocational training for the disabled; and
- involvement of NGOs in this work.

The Programme of Action (POA) states the placement principle: a child with disability who can be educated in the general school should not be in the special school. Even those children who are initially admitted to special schools for training in daily living skills plus curriculum skills should be integrated in general schools, once they acquire daily living skills, communication skills and basic academic skills. The POA, 1992 not only reiterated the principle of integration but also made it an integral component of all basic education projects: non-formal education, adult education, vocational education and teacher education schemes, funded by the central government.

Present Scenario

The Ministry of Welfare is the nodal ministry for the welfare of the handicapped. The special schools' sector is dealt with by the Ministry of Welfare whereas integrated education is being dealt with in the education sector. At present, only about 60,000 children receive education in about 1,400 special schools and about 50,000 disabled children are in the integrated education programme. This is against the estimated 10–15 million children with disabilities that require educational facilities.

As the present coverage of disabled children under the umbrella of education is not more than 1 per cent, the Working Group for the Welfare and Development of Persons with Disabilities has suggested systematic efforts to provide education to all of them by 2010 AD. Insofar as integrated education is concerned, it has recommended extension of this approach to 500 additional blocks in the Ninth Five Year Plan. The main recommendations of the Working Group are outlined in Appendix II.

The Persons with Disabilities (Equal Opportunities, Protection of Rights and Full Participation) Act, 1995 has also come into force recently. It has identified seven categories of disability, both physical and mental. Chapter 5 of the Act pertains to Education. It enjoins upon the government to ensure that every child with a disability has access to free education in an appropriate environment till the age of 18 years and inter alia provides for the establishment of special schools, facilities for imparting non-formal education and education through open schools/universities to disabled children, organising teacher training programmes, taking steps for adaptation of curriculum, reform of the examination system, promoting research and providing various facilities to the disabled children.

The Act places responsibility on the 'appropriate government' for implementing its various provisions. The onus, therefore, is apportioned between national, state and local governments. At the national level, the Ministry of Welfare is the nodal ministry for the welfare of the disabled. The chapter on 'Education' has relevance to this department. In this sector, while the special schools come under the purview of the Ministry of Welfare, the Department of Education has been making efforts to provide integrated education to disabled children with mild and moderate handicaps in normal schools. Since education is a concurrent subject and is under the administrative control of the state governments, the primary responsibility for education of the disabled has to be taken by the state government. The central government's role is to provide a catalyst and support the endeavours of the state government. The local bodies, the NGOs and all others concerned with education are equally responsible for implementation of the provisions of the Act.

Initiatives Taken by the Department of Education

Many of the aspects specified in the Act are being covered by the IEDC scheme entirely, particularly in respect of facilities for disabled children (Articles 27[f], 30[a–c]), and partly in respect of others. In addition, efforts have been made to incorporate the needs of disabled children in other ongoing programmes of the department.

Under the District Primary Education Programme (DPEP) launched in 1994 as a centrally sponsored scheme, integrated education for all children with mild to moderate disabilities is being given special emphasis. Financial parameters have been worked out and guidelines have been evolved for the purpose. As per the guidelines, DPEP will fund interventions for the integrated education of primary schoolgoing children through a process of environment building, community mobilisation and early detection; in-service teacher training; development of innovative designs for primary schools and removal of architectural barriers in existing schools; provision of educational aids and appliances; resource support at block/district level; placement of a programme officer at the DPEP district project office; establishment of an advisory resource group at the state level and apex level group at the national level for providing overall guidance; and technical and academic support to integrated education under DPEP. Already, awareness building has begun and one workshop on the subject has been conducted. Around 120 districts spread over 13 states have been covered under DPEP. Children with integrable disabilities are expected to be brought into the system in phases.

Under the Rajasthan Shiksha Karmi Project introduced in 1987, with the aim of universalisation and qualitative improvement of primary education in remote and socioeconomically backward villages in Rajasthan, 1,801 physically handicapped children have been enrolled. A special input is being incorporated in the training of Shiksha Karmis to enable them to take care of children suffering from mild to moderate disabilities. A study is also proposed to be commissioned to determine the special needs of such children and teacher training inputs in this regard.

Fee concessions are being provided to handicapped persons by the National Open School. The enrolment of handicapped persons in the various programmes was estimated at around 0.7 per cent in 1993–94.

To focus on the needs of the disabled children in adult literacy programmes, the State Resource Centre, Delhi will, in consultation with NCERT, work out a training capsule for teachers for imparting functional literacy skills to disabled non-literate persons.

A beginning has also been made by the University Grants Commission (UGC) for orienting universities/colleges to the needs of disabled children. The UGC is implementing a scheme under which financial assistance is provided, as per the prescribed norms, to universities for organising special education programmes for B.Ed./M.Ed. teachers, to enable them to teach disabled children. The number of universities/colleges currently being assisted under the scheme is 12. Also, the UGC has reserved 30 research associateships per annum for physically handicapped students.

With the objective of extending the benefit of vocational and technical training to the physically handicapped, two co-educational polytechnics for the physically handicapped are being set up in the states of Karnataka and Uttar Pradesh as part of the World Bank assisted Technician Education Project. While the one in Mysore (Karnataka) has already started functioning, the one in Kanpur (UP) is to be operationalised soon. The buildings for these polytechnics are planned in the light of the standards prevailing the world over for such institutes. Special equipment and furniture are being procured and special training arrangements are being made for the teachers. It is intended that these two polytechnics, along with the Technical Teachers Training Institute, will act as resource centres for teacher training, development of educational material, curricula and teaching aids for persons with disabilities.

In addition, under the centrally sponsored scheme of Vocationalisation of Secondary Education launched in 1987–88, assistance is being provided to NGOs for imparting non-formal, short term vocational training to school dropouts and unemployed youth. Special efforts have been made to enhance the involvement of NGOs working for the welfare of the disabled. Many such organisations are thus being funded under this scheme.

The Educational Consultants India Ltd. (Ed. Cil), which is one of the public sector undertakings under the Department of Education, is providing 3 per cent reservation for persons with disabilities as per the guidelines of the Department of Public Enterprises on the subject.

Although a modest beginning has been made to enhance access of disabled children to education, much more needs to be done to meet the requirements of the Act. The provisions of the Act are being further examined in consultation with NCERT and the Central Board of Secondary Education. In the Ninth Plan, it is proposed to substantially augment the resources under the IEDC and expand its coverage. Strategies are also being evolved to integrate the concerns of the disabled children more specifically in all the ongoing programmes of this department. In doing so, strong support from the welfare sector, particularly in providing aids and appliances, fostering research and providing training to various categories of functionaries through their National Institutes, will also be required.

Appendix I

Assistance to States/Union Territories for Integrated Education for Disabled Children (IEDC)

Name of the State/ Union Territory	Amount Released (Rs. in lakhs) (Plan)					
	1991–92	1992–93	1993–94	1994–95	1995–96	1996–97 (as on 29.11.96)
Andhra Pradesh			14.01	32.46		
Bihar		36.95		26.58		
Gujarat	34.50	67.21		39.50		28.01
Haryana		16.80				
Himachal Pradesh	7.21	9.55	6.34		3.90	
Jammu & Kashmir	16.69					
Karnataka	45.28	39.08	4.19	70.73	47.78	2.42
Kerala	77.54		125.28	66.59	495.21	
Madhya Pradesh		30.90		52.72		
	2.17 (VO)	2.49 (VO)	2.95 (VO)	3.29 (VO)	2.36 (VO)	1.72 (VO)
Manipur	3.98	5.00	22.40		8.40	5.72
Maharashtra			75.53	13.43 23.00 (VO)		17.05
Mizoram	31.72	45.36	1.92	14.00	11.51	
Nagaland	10.79	12.61	5.74	11.71	5.41	
Orissa	22.46	35.20	68.92	43.64	4.84	59.44

Punjab	12.00					1.10 (VO)
Rajasthan	71.14	28.33	85.35	26.25	20.20	
Tamil Nadu	9.90	28.41				
		0.62 (VO)	5.32 (VO)	4.14 (VO)	13.22 (VO)	
Tripura			2.01		0.87	
West Bengal					3.76	
				34.00 (VO)	12.00 (VO)	
A & N Islands	16.08	20.65	9.84	13.37	12.78	6.62
Chandigarh			0.99	0.99		
Delhi	16.14	0.03	18.74	37.50	4.54	
				1.25	2.18	
				(VO)	19.89 (VO)	
Daman & Diu	0.53	0.29	0.42	0.45	0.45	
Total	**378.13**	**379.48**	**449.95**	**516.94**	**670.00**	**122.66**
			i.e., 450.00	i.e., 517.00		

Note: VO stands for Voluntary Organisations.

Appendix II

Main Recommendations of the Working Group for the Welfare and Development of the Disabled, set up by the Ministry of Welfare for the Ninth Plan

The Working Group for the Welfare and Development of the Disabled and the Sub-group on the Disabled have already submitted their reports, with specific recommendations on education for the disabled. These include:

- integration in all ongoing national and state level programmes under EFA, including DPEP and adult education programmes;
- every district to have one fully equipped resource centre to meet the educational needs of all children with special needs;
- 1,200 special schools to be established during the Ninth Plan;
- integrated education, using the PIED approach, to be extended to 500 additional blocks;
- every state to have one school to serve children with multiple disabilities;
- 5 per cent of the total budget allocation for education at the central and state levels to be earmarked for children with special needs;

- the state governments should assume responsibility for the education of disabled children in both special schools and in integrated education programmes as a part of the general education programmes;
- the general teacher preparation programmes to include adequate input on special education in the curriculum;
- the national institutes for the handicapped, regional colleges of education, universities and VOs to be given specific targets for preparing the required number of specialist teachers and multi-category teachers in the Ninth Five Year Plan. Approximately 44,000 special teachers and multi-category teachers will be required for the targetted 25 per cent of children with special needs to be covered under the Ninth Plan; and
- The salary structure and service conditions of special teachers to be commensurate with that of general classroom teachers, as applicable in the respective state governments.

Adequate emphasis to be given to research in the field of special education, vocational training and rehabilitation with at least 5 per cent of the allocation for special education to be set aside for this purpose.

2

Special Needs Policy in India

Mithu Alur

Introduction

A few years ago I started examining a particular policy of the Government of India known as the Integrated Child Development Scheme (ICDS) which does not include children with special needs in its provision of services. The ICDS operates amongst the poorest sections of the population, amongst people living in the peri-urban slums of inner cities, in peripheral tribal and hilly areas, and in the rural villages of India. It is a unique initiative which evolved from the National Policy for Children, providing a package of services to children below the age of six, as well as to expectant and nursing mothers. The services include health check-ups, immunisation and nutrition, referral services and informal preschool services (Sood, 1987). Today the ICDS is considered to be the world's largest package of services for woman and child. A programme which began with three projects, has now grown to 2,600 centres reaching out to the weakest and most vulnerable sectors of the country (Siraj-Blatchford, 1994; Swaminathan, 1992). However, relevant to my investigation, the ICDS policy does not include children with special needs.

Therefore, my question has been: why has the ICDS excluded children with special needs from its service provisions? How is India going to be able to achieve 'Education for All' if children with special needs are not brought into existing services? This chapter, therefore, tracks the evolution of social policy in India in the last 50 years during the post-Independence period, and examines three major policies of government that have developed in the post-Independence era. It concludes by analysing various factors that have contributed to the disabled still remaining excluded from government provisions.

Policy issues are rooted in a wider socioeconomic and political context, generally catering to the needs of the wider society. It has been said that 'Policy analysis is finding out what governments do, why they do it and what difference it makes' (Dye, 1976). It was in order to establish the rationale for the exclusion of children with special needs that I began this study with an examination of the evolution of policy for people with disabilities in India in a broader context.

The Context

Historical: A Pre-Independence Overview of Education for the Handicapped

Historically, organised attempts to educate blind children were made in India when Christian missionaries established schools. The first school for blind children was established by an English missionary known as Annie Sharp in Amritsar in 1887. Interestingly enough, throughout the nineteenth century, an unknown number of blind children were casually integrated with sighted children, picking up whatever they could from oral repetition, which was the major tool of pedagogy. Priscilla Chapman remarked on a blind girl in Calcutta in 1826, who 'from listening to the other children got by heart the Gospel' (Chapman, 1839, as mentioned in Miles, 1996).

Due to insufficient documentation, researchers in the past 50 years, both Indian and foreign, are poorly informed about India's special educational needs and disability issues in the nineteenth century. Until about 1947, the then provincial governments had taken sporadic interest in the education and training of the handicapped, usually by giving ad hoc grants to schools and other institutions for the handicapped, and it emerges that it was voluntary effort that played a pioneering role in the field of education and social service (Gupta, 1984).

In 1994 in England, the Education Act or the Butler Act was passed universalising education. At about the same time in India, in 1944, the

Central Advisory Board of Education (CABE) published a comprehensive report on the post-war educational development of the country, popularly known as the Sargent Report. In this report, provisions for the handicapped were to form an essential part of the national system of education and were to be administered by the education department. Whenever possible, the report stated, handicapped children should not be segregated from normal children. Only when the nature and extent of their defect make it necessary, should they be sent to special schools (Sargent Report, 1944: Chapter IX, pp. 76–82). The CABE Report goes on to point out that governments in India, whether central or provincial, had shown little interest in this subject and had left it almost entirely to voluntary effort (ibid.).

1. Provision for the mentally or physically handicapped should form an essential part of a national system of education and should be administered by the education department.
2. Hitherto in India, governments have hardly interested themselves at all in this branch of education; what has been done has been due almost entirely to voluntary effort.
3. Wherever possible, handicapped children should not be segregated from normal children. Only when the nature and extent of their defect make it necessary, should they be sent to special schools or institutions. Partially handicapped children should receive special treatment at ordinary schools.
4. Particular care should be taken to train the handicapped, wherever possible, for remunerative employment and to find such employment for them. After-care work is essential.
5. In the absence of any reliable data it is impossible to estimate what would be the cost of making adequate provision for the handicapped in India; 10 per cent of the total expenditure on basic and high schools has been set aside for special services, which include such provision, and it is hoped that this will suffice (Sargent Report, 1944: Chapter 9, p. 82).

We see, therefore, that the board was guided by the fundamental principle that children with disabilities should not, if it can possibly be helped, be segregated from normal children; only when the nature or extent of their defect makes it necessary should they be sent to special schools or institutions.

Here is a Charter in 1944, which is not debating inclusion, but it is taken that this is the way it should be done. Debate and discourse should only have been on **how** it should be done. What happened since then?

Post-Independence Scenario

The Kothari Commission, 1964–1966

In 1964, the Kothari Commission was the first education commission which brought up the issue of children with special needs in the Plan of Action (Gupta, 1984; Jangira, 1995) and again gave strong recommendations for including children with special needs into ordinary schools.

> We now turn to the education of handicapped children. Their education has to be organised not merely on humanitarian grounds of utility. Proper education generally enables a handicapped child to overcome largely his or her handicap and make him into a useful citizen. Social justice also demands it.
>
> It must be remembered that the Constitutional directive on compulsory education includes handicapped children as well.
>
> There is much in the field that we could learn from the educationally advanced countries which in recent years have developed new methods and techniques, based on advances in science and medicine.
>
> On an overall view of the problem, however, we feel that experimentation with integrated programmes is urgently required and every attempt should be made to bring in as many children in integrated programmes.

The Commission further recommended that:

> The Ministry of Education should allocate the necessary funds and NCERT should establish a cell for the study of handicapped children. The principal function of the cell would be to keep in touch with the research that is being done in the country and abroad and to prepare materials for teachers.

Therefore, while reviewing Government of India documents created during the post-Independence period, one finds that services for children with special needs seem to have followed the pattern of segregation, although statements of intent show otherwise. The rhetoric remains on paper and not in practice.

I now move on to examine how this could have happened, examining what has been the practice during these 53 years since Independence. To do this I analyse three policies of the Government of India.

Policy of Assistance to Voluntary Organisations, Ministry of Welfare

In June 1964, work concerning the education, training and rehabilitation of the handicapped was transferred from the Ministry of Education to a newly created Department of Social Security. This department became the Ministry of Social Welfare (GOI, 1965). This happened despite the CABE Report and the Report of the Kothari Commission which had recommended that children with disabilities should be a part of the mainstream system. The Ministry of Welfare as it became known in the 1980s was entrusted with the responsibility for the welfare of the scheduled classes, other backward classes, drug addicts, cancer patients, those affected with leprosy, women and children, and children with special needs—a heterogeneous group of people who constitute the most vulnerable and weakest segments of the population, and form over half of India's population.

Since the commencement of the Second Plan (1956–1961), the union government continued the same paternalistic practice of the provincial governments of the pre-Independence period of doling out grants to voluntary organisations. Thus, government policy towards children with special needs was, and still is, principally dependent on voluntary organisations to deliver minimal micro level services.

Today major work is done by the voluntary sector. There are over 2,500 organisations in the field. About 450 of these organisations get grants from the Ministry of Welfare towards their operational costs (GOI, 1990; Gupta, 1984; Jangira, 1995). Special schools exist for the blind, deaf, cerebral palsied, mentally handicapped and slow learners, very similar to what was happening in England in 1944 when there was rigid labelling and categorisation of disabled people. A larger number of NGOs sustain activities through their own funding efforts and in partnership with international partners.

The government's assistance in the way of grants-in-aid to voluntary organisations has become officially the accepted state policy as far as children with special needs are concerned, with no direct link between the state and the child...no obligations, no rights.

Policy of Integration,
Ministry of Human Resource Development

In 1975, the government introduced Project Integrated Education for the Disabled (PIED). This scheme, previously with the Ministry of Welfare, was transferred to the Ministry of HRD, under the IEDC Scheme. Children in the age group 5 to 14 with not so severe impairments as determined through medical assessment were to be eligible for admission in regular schools. Through PIED, integration of a large number of children has happened.

Aggarwal, reviewing current developments in education, writes that 28,000 children spread over 6,000 schools are presently receiving benefits under this scheme. A much larger number are receiving indirect benefit through special teachers and other learning materials (Aggarwal, 1992).

According to Miles (1985), the number of children with special needs in ordinary schools far exceeds the number of children with special needs in special schools. The fact that there are states which do not have any special schools has no doubt helped 'casual integration' to take place.

On the whole, the findings indicate that India has the largest number of children with special needs integrated into ordinary schools in the Asia region and, due to the paucity of special schools round the country, an amount of casual and unplanned integration is already taking place, though no major study has been done about the efficacy of this integration (World Bank, 1994). This undoubtedly will help the question of inclusive education.

Again, of late there has been a significant trend towards integration. India has been a signatory in the Salamanca Conference held in Spain on 'Education for All'. In June 1994, representatives of 92 Governments and 25 international organisations signed a resolution which was a dynamic new statement on the education of all disabled children. In pursuance of the Salamanca Conference 'Education for All', the Government of India has launched the District Primary Education Programme (DPEP) where children with special needs are to be integrated into ordinary schools. The DPEP is expected to examine teacher training, curriculum modification, resource room support and teacher support. The Ministry of Social Justice and Empowerment, in the Indian Eigth Five Year Plan, 1991–1996, increased the budget for children with impairments by more than five times (DPEP Programme, 1993). With the establishment of the DPEP programme, India has taken a step forward in its policy of inclusion.

However, the finding shows that the issue of integration is sporadic and based on individual initiatives, and not taking place as an organised programme of the state. The continuance of state-supported special schools certainly brings sharply into focus the contradictory government approaches in maintaining special schools as well as in attempting to integrate children with special needs into the regular school system in a piecemeal fashion.

Policy of Integrated Child Development Scheme, Ministry of Human Research Development

In 1974, the government launched the Integrated Child Development Scheme. This programme is supposedly the world's largest package of services for the most vulnerable sections of the population (Swaminathan, 1992). However, disabled under-fives are not admitted in the anganwadi and balwadis, nor is the family given any support system, and when asked why they do not attend the ICDS clinics, the mothers seem embarrassed and say 'No, that is not for us'. The anganwadi workers too confirm that there is no place for disabled children and its not their job.

Since the ICDS works in the slums, the tribal and rural areas, it is the most appropriate service to include disabled children, who are mainly amongst the most vulnerable sections of society. Yet, professionals associated with early childhood care, while designing manuals and curriculum for training of para-professionals in early learning, have not included preschool disabled children.

The policy makers too are aware of the critical 0–5 years and a large resource allocation has been made to the ICDS; yet children with special needs are not included in this so-called integrated package concerning even basic needs such as health, nutrition and preschool facilities.

Clearly such a major social policy in the country has left out disability from their agenda. The argument usually proffered by policy makers is that the para-professional workers are overloaded and have no knowledge of how to handle a handicapped child.

Therefore, although provisions are made for the scheduled castes, the poor, women and children, the disabled get identified as a separate category and remain marginalised. Hence, the disabled child, the disabled woman and the disabled person from a scheduled caste and tribe do not benefit from the concessions granted to their groups. Although they are an impoverished disadvantaged and are entitled to some services being given by the government, the disabled within this group are excluded from basic health care methods.

According to various writers, consideration needs to be given at all levels in the implementation of policy. The front line people or service delivery workers and policy implementers, such as teachers, nurses, police officers, health and community workers, have been called 'street level bureaucrats' (Lipsky, 1980). Street level bureaucrats have enormous powers and usually enjoy considerable autonomy. Research shows that they can be highly discretionary and are essentially exclusionary. To study the inequities that exist in the Indian situation, Figure 2.1 shows the link

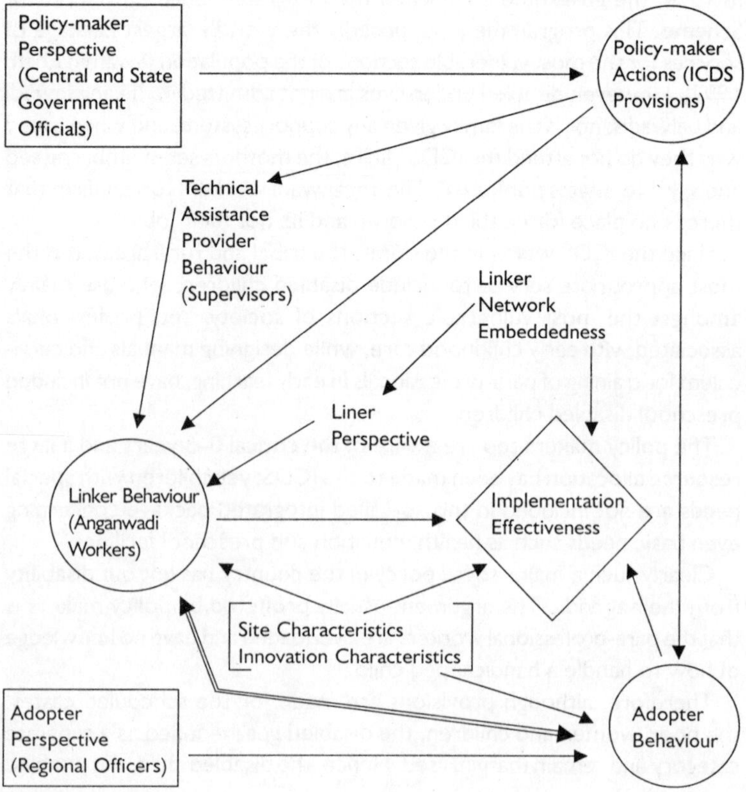

Figure 2.1: Showing the linkage in policy and implementation

in the ICDS policy between policy makers and the street level bureaucrats, in this case the anganwadi workers and their supervisors of the ICDS policy. Clarity is needed in any policy if it is to be put into implementation. The primary concern of the anganwadi workers and supervisors being to manage their workloads, there will be serious distortions of actual policy. The fundamental flaw in a top-down model is that it starts from the central actors, and tends to neglect other actors specially on the ground level.

The policy implementation process operates continuously, involving many levels of people on the central government level, on a local government level, concerning local policy and priorities; or at the level of administrators and professionals (Goacher et al., 1988; Hill, 1993).

It has been suggested that street level bureaucrats will continue developing arbitrary norms of behaviour unless (a) the actual policy of including the child with special needs is spelt out clearly, and (b) they are taught how to deal with them (Lipsky, 1980).

Legislation

The Persons with Disability Act

One of the major pieces of legislation that has attempted to codify provisions to the disabled has been the Persons With Disability Act. According to the Act, it is now the responsibility of the local government to ensure that every child with disability, from any part of the country, will have access to free education until the age of eighteen. Integration in normal schools will be promoted, and appropriate authorities will be asked to make the necessary financial allocations for this purpose.

Briefly, it is now binding on the government through this new legislation to provide integrated education to children with special needs in the least restrictive environment.

However, the criticism has been that the legislation has no sponsor. It is a pious intent, looking at housing, access, employment, even recreation. A virtual utopia has been promised but with no mechanism or resources to implement it. Initiatives to promote legislative provisions for persons with disabilities have a difficulty. As Alston rightfully said, 'rights without mechanisms to claim and without obligation to provide are empty' (quoted in Harris-White, 1995a).

Since the education ministry is examining integration, it is logical that provisions for education should become the responsibility of the Ministry of Education.

An Analysis of Policy and Implementation

Lack of Commitment and Political Will

Historically, what becomes clear is that, although the Government's Statement of Intent exists, right from 1944, about the need to integrate children with disability into the existing system of education, the policy or practice following such Intent is not there. Because of the contradictions and ambiguities in administration, the roles of the different ministries get blurred and the government's statements on the subject have not helped to legitimise services as a matter of state provision, of entitlement and right.

Lack of Political Lobby

Basically, no government works without pressure. The policy process we have seen is a political process. It is an acceptable fact that political lobby plays a critical role in shaping and implementing policy (Barton, 1984; Hill, 1993; Kirp, 1982; Slee, 1993).

Since Independence, as we have seen, the disabled have been classified with other vulnerable and weaker sections of the population, such as women and children, the scheduled castes and scheduled tribes. Both these groups have had powerful political support. The scheduled castes have had a strong and persistent lobby built up by Mahatma Gandhi and Dr Ambedkar. They are powerful political groupings which represent 20 per cent of the population today. A weaker group, but which has also been very vociferous and visible today, is the women's group. Since Independence, they have formed various commissions and national committees, and various groups have emerged and been able to establish their rights and their status and representation in Parliament. Now there are proposed provisions to enhance the representation of women in Parliament to 33 per cent. Amongst the categories of people classified as vulnerable sections in the Constitution, the disabled group have the weakest lobby.

Dichotomy between Policy and Practice

We find that although the government continues its policy of integration, on a parallel level it continues its segregationary policy of promoting the idea of special schools through its assistance to voluntary organisations schemes (via the Ministry of Welfare). This produces a dichotomy not in keeping with the declared policy of 'Education for All', resulting in ambiguities, serious contradictions and blurring of intention, which will naturally be affecting policy on the ground level.

Voluntary not State

Work for the handicapped is still considered 'good' and humanitarian acts of charity. This has not helped the philosophy of rights or entitlement and obligation of the state.

Micro not Macro

Undoubtedly, the voluntary sector has played a very active and vigorous role in introducing new concepts of education and services, but without continuous funding and good infrastructural support, continued dependence on the government, with very limited and fast dwindling funds, has ensured that its activities are on a micro level. Today, because of the state's lack of involvement, a vast majority, over 90 per cent (according to recent government surveys) of the disabled remain outside the ambit of any service from the state.

Professionalism

There has been a school of thought that professionals may be specialised in their own area, but have clung their specialisation and created a mystique around them for their own vested interests (Barnes, 1990; Barton and Tomlinson, 1984; Tomlinson, 1982). According to sociologist and writer, Sally Tomlinson: 'The rhetoric of special needs may be humanitarian, the practice is controlled by vested interests' (Tomlinson, 1982: 73–75). She has gone on to term this as 'benevolent humanitarianism', professionals being the benefactors and clients the weaker members of society. It has been written that this group in modern society seems to be the authority to interpret normality and abnormality…a group that seems to have accumulated the power to define and classify others as normal and abnormal and to treat their body and their minds (Foucault, 1987; Skrtic, 1991a: 22; Wilding, 1982: 3).

These views are very relevant to the charitable work being done by a large body of voluntary workers in India. Children with special needs are in special schools run by people who know best and are doing good for the children with their 'deficiencies' (Abberley, 1987; Mason, 1992; Oliver, 1988). This is a major drawback in the process of integration.

Special Education needs to be demystified. At present, it is too esoteric and guarded by a small group. The government has thought it best to make this their policy and allow this state of affairs to continue.

Depoliticisation and Individualisation

To look merely for technical solutions rather than examine political or structural issues is a means which has been called depoliticisation of a situation (Vincent et al., 1996; Wilding, 1982). Depoliticisation of situations and individualising children and families as suffering from private troubles locates the problem outside the public sphere of concern (Barton and Oliver, 1995; Tomlinson, Fulcher, 1984).

Here in India, powerful professionals, well placed and well educated, have no doubt introduced considerable technical skills into the work for people with disabilities. However, the work has been fragmented and isolated, moving away from the rights and entitlement issues to an individual problem. Mainly being services organisations, the NGOs working for different categories of disabled children, with their own interests of providing services and support to the category they are serving, have contributed to fragmentation and weakness in the political arena.

Changing government policy, and empowering disabled people and their families to lobby for their rights, which is the most critical thinking in the developed countries today, is also not part of their agenda, adding to the continued political weakness of disabled people.

Conclusion

A 'conceptual fragmentation' has taken place creating a dichotomy in the Indian situation, creating the divergent agendas and a lack of cohesion in the provision of services within the two ministries, Welfare and HRD. Therefore, analysing the current scenario, while we are making sporadic attempts in inclusive education, we are nowhere near EFA.

In the last 50 years, no step has been taken to create a uniform policy for children with special needs, widening the gap between the State's Statement of Intent and actual provision of service on the ground level. This confused, blur and contextual mass of contradictions and ambiguities seem to be underpinning social policy for children with special needs in India.

The Need of the Hour

- This dichotomy between intent and practice must be removed urgently, if we are to meet the challenges ahead for UPE and EFA.
- To this end, India urgently needs to examine the impediments that are coming in the way of universalising education. Culture-specific paradigms need to be innovated by NGOs. The HRD ministry, with its various arms, such as NCERT, NCTE, NIEPA, NIPCED, needs to seriously study the problem and move the education of children with special needs into its own sphere.
- This policy needs to percolate to all government departments, including a policy like the ICDS.
- The voluntary sector too needs to redefine its objectives and slowly desegregate its segregated outfits, moving towards integration and equalisation of opportunities for its clients.
- The parents of disabled children and professionals should also show vigour in meeting the challenge as, during the transition period, we should bear in mind that integration is a long journey and not a path strewn with roses.

Policy implementation has been described as a multi-dimensional model with layers like onions overlapping, and each layer coming in contact with the other and influencing the other. Figure 2.2 shows the different levels that need to be addressed. The outer layer shows the wider question of policy and implementation involving government bureaucrats, administrators, professionals; the next few layers narrow into the community, the family surrounding the child within the environment. The arrows show the services on the ground level, which could be a special school or an inclusive school or, as is usually the case with the majority of disabled under five, no school at all due to lack of clarity in policy.

Figure 2.2: A diagrammatic matrix indicating the levels of areas to be investigated within the options available for the disabled child

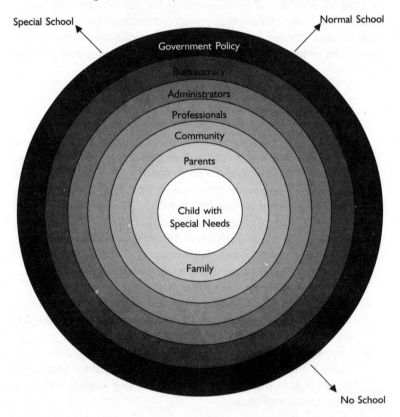

Tracking policy and practice, one must bear in mind that the dichotomy that exists in practice is not merely a dichotomy between policy and practice, but a failure to implement the Intent, an Intent that has been accepted by the government ever since 1944, showing a lack of political will and an ideological commitment.

References

Abberley, P. (1987) 'The Concept of Oppression and the Development of a Social Theory of Disability', *Disability, Handicap and Society*, 2(1): 5–19.

Aggarwal, J.C. (1992) *Education Policy in India—Retrospect and Prospect*. New Delhi: Shipra.

Barton, L. (1984) *The Politics of Special Education Needs*. Lewes: Falmer Press.

Barton, L. and **M. Oliver** (1995) *Power and Partnership in Education*. London: Routledge.

Barton, L. and **S. Tomlinson** (eds) (1984) *Special Education and Social Interests*. London: Croon Helm.

Chapman, P. (1839) 'Hindoo Family Education', in M. Miles (1996).

District Primary Education Programme (DPEP) (1994) *DPEP Guidelines*. New Delhi: Ministry of Human Resource Development.

Dye, T.R. (1976) *Understanding Public Policy*, 4th edn. Englewood Cliffs, NJ: Prentice-Hall.

Foucault, M. (1987) 'Mental Illness and Psychology.' Translated by Alan Sheridan. First edn. New York: Harper & Row.

Fulcher, G. (1990) 'Students with Special Needs: Lessons From Comparisons', *Journal of Education Policy*, 5: 347–58.

Goacher, B., J. Evans, J. Welton and **K. Wedell** (1988) *Policy and Provisions for Special Education Needs: Implementing the 1981 Education Act*. London: Cassell.

Government of India (1965a) Kothari Commission. Report of the Education Commission, Education and National Development. New Delhi: Ministry of Education.

——— (1965b) *Education in Eighteen Years of Freedom*. New Delhi: Ministry of Education.

Gupta, S.K. (1984) 'A Study of Special Needs Provisions for the Education of Children with Visual Handicaps in England and Wales and in India.' Associateship Study, Institute of Education, University of London.

Harriss-White, B. (1995a) *On to A Loser: Disability in India*. Paper available with author at Elizabeth House, Development Studies, Oxford University, Oxford.

——— (1995b) *The Political Economy of Disability and Development with Special Reference to India*. Paper available at Elizabeth House, Development Studies, Oxford University, Oxford.

Hill, M. (ed.) (1993) *The Policy Process: A Reader*. New York, London: Harvester Wheatsheaf.

Jangira, N.K. (1995) 'Rethinking Teacher Education', *Prospects*, 25(2): 261–72.

Kirp, D. (1982) 'Professionalisation as a Policy Choice, British Special Ed. in Comparative Perspective', *Journal of World Politics*, 34(2): 137–75.

Lipsky, M. (1980) 'Street-Level Bureaucracy: An Introduction', in M. Hill (ed.) *The Policy Process: A Reader*. London: Harvester Wheatsheaf.

Mason, M. (1992) 'The Integration Alliance: Background and Manifesto', in T. Booth, W. Swann, M. Masterson and P. Potts (eds) *Policies for Diversity in Education*. London: Open University/Routledge.

Miles, M. (1985) 'Children with Disabilities in Ordinary Schools. An Action Study of Non-Designed Educational Integration in Pakistan'. Peshawar: Mental Health Centre for National Council of Social Welfare, Government of Pakistan.

——— (1996) 'Community, Individual or Information Development? Dilemmas of Concept and Culture in South Asian Disability Planning', *Disability & Society*, 11(4): 485–500.

Oliver, M. (1988) 'The Social and Political Context of Education Policy', in L. Barton (ed.) *The Policy of Special Educational Needs*. London: Falmer Press.

Sargent, J. (1944) *Society, Schools, and Progress in India*. Oxford: Pergamon Press.

Siraj-Blatchford, I. (1994) 'An Evaluation of Early Years Education and Training in the ICDS in India', *International Journal of Early Years Education*, 2(1): 63.

Skrtic, T.M. (1991a) *Behind Special Education: A Critical Analysis of Professional Culture and School Organisation*. Denver, Colo.: Love.

———— (1991b) 'Students with Special Educational Needs: Artifacts of the Traditional Curriculum', in M. Ainscow (ed.) *Effective Schools for All*. London: David Fulton.

Slee, R. (ed.) (1993) *Is There A Desk With My Name On It?* London: Falmer Press.

Sood, N. (1987) 'An Evaluation of Non Formal Preschool Education Component in Mangolpuri ICDS block', *NIPCCD Technical Bulletin*, 1 April.

Swaminathan, M. (1992) *The Coordinators, Training Child Care Workers in India*. UNICEF, Issue 12.

Tomlinson, S. (1982) *A Sociology of Special Education*. London: Routledge & Kegan Paul.

———— (1984) *A Sociology of Special Education*. London: Routledge & Kegan Paul.

Vincent, C., J. Evans, I. Lunt and **P. Young** (1996) 'Professionals Under Pressure: The Administration of Special Education in a Changing Context', *British Educational Research Journal*, 22(4): 475–91.

Wilding, P. (1982) *Professional Power and Social Welfare*. London: Routledge & Kegan Paul.

World Bank (1994) 'Provision for Children with Special Educational Needs in the Asia Region', World Bank Technical Paper, No. 261. Hampshire, England: Microinfo Ltd.

3

Special Educational Needs of Children and Young Adults: An Unfinished Agenda

N.K. Jangira

The education of children and young adults with special educational needs has not yet been addressed as a human rights issue in most developing countries, despite constitutional commitments to universal basic education. It continues to be treated as a residual item in educational plans and is the last priority to be addressed, or is addressed in a marginal way. The failure to develop a sizeable human resource is untenable not only as an equity and human rights issue, but also from the point of view of sustainable economic development. Let us take stock of achievements briefly, identify gaps and the unfinished agenda, and specify steps toward inclusive education.

Achievements

One must acknowledge the positive developments that have taken place in most developing countries during the last decade and a half with the declaration of the International Year of Disabled Persons in 1981 and the Jomtien Conference on Education for All in 1990. Awareness of the special educational needs of persons with disabilities and in other difficult circumstances has increased due to strong advocacy and communication initiatives. Modalities of provision, however, still continue to be problematic. Many countries have enacted legislation and increased resource allocation. Programmes for integration of children and young adults with disabilities in corporate community life, education and economic activities have been initiated. Including the integration of children with special educational needs in the District Primary Education Programme in India is a positive signal for scaling up implementation. Increased global resources and technical support are available to countries in need to stimulate programmes in this area. I am referring here to trends which can be observed and not commenting on their sufficiency or quality, though I believe the trends are encouraging.

Gaps

Inclusive schooling implies schools which have been organised to meet the educational needs of all children in the communities they serve. All children, including children with special educational needs, have access to the curriculum in such schools. Teaching is organised to meet the increased range of student needs. Curriculum flexibility and school and classroom organisation allow adaptation to meet diverse student needs. The concept is equally applicable to other educational institutions. The enabling conditions for inclusive education are:

- common administrative structure for special and regular education,
- resource support to meet special educational needs, and
- adaptation of curriculum, teaching and assessment to needs of all children, including those with special educational needs.

A number of gaps and shortfalls in provision can be identified in the light of an inclusive education perspective (UNESCO, 1994).

Knowledge Gap

Policy makers, planners and administrators are aware of the need for educating children and young adults with special educational needs in terms of both human rights and the development of human resources. They are, however, unclear about the nature and modalities of provision in the context of educational development in their own countries. For example, they subscribe to the concept of 'integration' which emerged from developed systems which have 'segregated' special education institutions. For developed systems it is a qualitative change from segregated education to integration. Developing countries are late starters in special education and the disadvantage of late start can be converted into an advantage by supporting reform of the existing regular school system to meet the educational needs of all children. It is an integral part of the overall strategy to improve the quality and efficiency of the regular education system. Inclusive education provides the basis for such a reform. Inclusive education is an alternative for developed education systems but it is an inevitability for developing systems (Jangira, 1995).

Policy and Implementation Disconnection

There is always some gap between policy and its implementation in social sectors due to the complexity of institutional dynamics and human development, but the gap found in relation to the education of children and young adults with special educational needs is somewhat disturbing. For example, legislation has been enacted but implementation within a reasonable time-frame remains elusive. The National Policy on Education and the Programme of Action for its implementation in 1986 and Revised Policy Formulations in 1992 made several useful recommendations. What is the status of implementation? In the development of DIETs, provision to support integration of children with special needs is the first casualty despite its inclusion in the scheme. The same is the case with regard to the implementation of the scheme for institutes of advanced study of education. Use of special schools as resource centres to support regular schools to meet special educational needs still remains only a paper recommendation, maybe due to the dual administration of special education.

Dual Administration

In several countries, special education still remains with departments other than education (Hegarty, 1988). For example, in India special schools and other related institutions are administered by the Ministry of Social Welfare, while integrated education for children with special educational needs is administered by the Department of Education in the Ministry of Human Resource Development. Fuller utilisation of the resources in special and regular education institutions is still to be achieved. The first enabling condition for inclusive education is violated. Children with special educational needs do not have equal educational opportunities on account of the limitations of special schools, and teachers do not get the same compensation as their counterparts in regular schools. In the absence of norms for expenditure and grants, most special schools remain starved of the required facilities. The exclusion of these children from the scheme of universal basic education for so long is the glaring example of this disconnection.

Dysfunctional Convergence and Coordination Mechanism

The education of children and young adults with special educational needs requires inputs from different sectors—social support from the welfare sector, early identification, stimulation and care inputs from the women and child development sector, medical and health assessment and rehabilitation assistance from the health sector. The co-ordinating mechanisms at different levels, particularly at the district and subdistrict levels, are inadequate. It makes the convergence of services problematic. The concept of shifting centrality of responsibility has yet to be operationalised. For example, in education, education department responsibility is central and other sectors provide support to facilitate it. In health, the education sector will play a supportive role for education and communication regarding health messages in the communities. Parallel systems are costly and less efficient. Co-ordinating mechanisms at the central and state level do not percolate down to the grass roots level which is the real scene of action.

Central and State Commitment Disconnection

The education of children with special educational needs is still considered a central responsibility. Otherwise, what is the justification for states to discontinue the centrally sponsored scheme of Integrated Education for Disabled Children (IEDC) launched by the Ministry of Welfare in 1974 as soon as it was converted into a 50–50 matching scheme in 1979? The states are reluctant to fund support teachers from the post-NPE period of the IEDC, and special school funding is mostly left for the NGOs in major states. The commitment of states and the centre to the human agenda has yet to emerge. The awaited legislation to make elementary education a fundamental right as suggested by the Supreme Court may serve as a catalyst to this kind of commitment. States have to own responsibility for this initiative.

Imbalance in Resource Allocation and Use

The effectiveness of the programme must be judged by the proportion of expenditures reaching the end beneficiaries, in this case children and young adults with special educational needs. The proportion of the resources expended on the structures and super specialisation is much higher in this area than what is spent on making provision. For example, the budget support for national institutes for the handicapped is much more than what is available for special schools and regular schools. The delivery system is top heavy, which results in shrinking actual resources available for the end beneficiary. It is true for the IEDC scheme as well. NIHs (National Institute for the Handicapped) do a lot of work which is the legitimate responsibility of health (association, rehabilitation), women and child development (early identification and stimulation), labour (vocational training) and education (training of teachers, education materials) departments. With convergence, rationalisation of responsibilities, giving priority to appropriate, technology-based programmes and need-based targeting of resources, many more beneficiaries can be served.

Resource-starved Programme

The education of children with special needs has always been a forgotten component of universal education plans. Allocations have mostly been nominal and ad hoc. Allocations proportionate to population have never been considered, as has happened with several other disadvantaged groups. Executive orders for the allocation of 3 per cent of the budget are being issued, probably based on incidence of disability. The education department is taking the lead. This allocation should be used for supporting inclusive education. These are the issues about the quantum of allocations and their use. For example, the needs of this group have been neglected for almost five decades since Independence and this has created a huge backlog. Should the mandatory allocation for children with special educational needs not be more than what is determined by their proportion in the population? If so, how much? Who will carry out advocacy for this? Will states also make provision for the mandatory allocations in their plans and budgets? Will it be applicable to all departments and all schemes at different levels of education that have to support inclusive education? What will be the mechanism for monitoring and enforcing the mandate? It also requires comprehensive planning involving the relevant sectors.

Reservation about Scaling of Innovations

There is no dearth of innovative work and experience in this area in India. There is experience of special schooling, integrated education and even inclusive schooling (carried out as a multi-site action research project by NCERT), community-based rehabilitation in NGOs as well as in government-supported institutions. There is, however, hesitation to go scale, maybe due to the constraint of resources, or low priority, accorded to the education of this group of students. Without scaling the goal of 'Education for All', equal opportunity for enhancing the quality of life in the national contexts cannot be realised.

Sidestepping Special Educational Needs in Curriculum Reform

The curriculum is basically textbook driven. The professed flexibility eludes school practice. Curriculum reforms have always sidestepped the need for adaptations for special educational needs. Due to dual administrative control of education of children with special needs, there are two sets of curricula, one for children in special schools (schools for the hearing impaired) and one for those in regular schools. Multi-level teaching and responsiveness to individual needs are yet to be included in curriculum transactions. Similarly, training programmes for teachers include little on the adaptation of instructional materials and methods for special needs.

Rigid Assessment and Examination Regime

The assessment and evaluation systems are examination-oriented and rigid. There is some provision for scribes for the blind and for certain other disability groups. The adaptation of goals, tools, medium and methodology of assessment are grey areas. There is little guidance material for teachers and very little provision is available in teacher training programmes. The yearly class system of curriculum coverage and promotion is made to apply to children with special educational needs as is done for all children. Diverse needs are not taken into consideration.

Programme of Action—The Way Ahead

Political Will and Commitment with Accountability

Political will and commitment are required for inclusive education for children and young adults with special educational needs under EFA and other education skill training programmes for all. The plans and allocations should not be based on incidence but on prevalence of special educational needs, taking into consideration the backlog created due to decades of neglect. The political commitment should come from the central government, the Parliament and the National Development Council. The Planning Commission and state governments should specify targeted resource allocation. The political commitment should be for accountability for result-oriented implementation and an effective monitoring mechanism to address it adequately as human rights and development issues.

Review of Implementation Focus

The focus now should shift from scheme or project mode to programme mode. There should be an emphasis on implementation with a bottom-up approach, school-based interventions dovetailed with regular education programmes following inclusive education strategies which are based on stakeholder participation and community mobilisation, mobilisation of NGOs, private and government resources. Regular reviews should be based on the performance indicators specified in the implementation programme.

Unified Educational Administration

Special education should be brought under a unified administration. Education is education, be it of children with special educational needs or other children. Education departments should own responsibility for managing education of all children, including those with special educational needs. The Ministry of Welfare should confine itself to support activities only. Integration of special and regular schools to support each other as envisaged in the Revised Policy Formulation on Education, 1992 (GOI, 1992) is the most important enabling condition for organising inclusive education.

Proportionate Resource Allocation for Access and Quality

At the expense of being repetitive, I suggest not only proportionate funding in all sectors and subsectors, but reiterate higher compensatory central and state allocations taking into account the years of neglect of special educational needs. The Ninth Plan should make a provision for support to inclusive education in all subsectors of education. The state plans should also make provision for this component as a part of education reform. This investment should not be perceived narrowly in terms of the number of special educational needs beneficiaries, but should be considered in a broader frame as it will improve the quality of education for all children. Against this perspective, additional funding will not look prohibitive, as is usually believed by the purse holders. For example, training of teachers in skills to adapt curriculum and assessment to individual needs, skills to organise multilevel teaching and classroom management to accommodate diverse needs would benefit all children and not just those with special educational needs.

Maximising Resources for Services to the End User

Resources on structures and new institutions should be reduced. Similarly, instead of concentrating on highly specialised skills and hiring costly specialists, multi-skilled support professionals should be developed. Capacity building inputs in the existing regular structures, institutions and persons should leave funding to reach large numbers of beneficiaries. Unified administration and inclusive schooling should be helpful. Much can be achieved with marginal additional inputs.

Plan and Implement Inclusive Schooling as System Reform

A professional group should be constituted to review the special and integrated programmes. The group should prepare a plan for curriculum and teacher education; reform, identify and develop an inclusive education support strategy; and cost the plan to be included in the Ninth Plan.

Special education is basically good quality education. Already special education has contributed a lot to regular education and teaching methodology. The complementarity will strengthen inclusive education to make it effective. The Teacher Education Resource Pack provides good material for classroom practice (UNESCO, 1993).

Integrate Available Experience and Scale-up Inclusive Schooling

India is not new to the concepts of special education, integration of special educational needs in regular schools and inclusive education. Several small scale experiments will be presented in the conferences in Mumbai, Delhi and Jaipur. Here I would refer to two experiments carried out by NCERT with funding from the GOI, UNESCO and UNICEF. Project Integrated Education for Disabled involved ten blocks in as many states, each block representing a unique context (scattered population in hilly and desert terrain, coastal area, tribal area, a responsive and a difficult administration, having support structures from relevant department and school-alone situation). External evaluation has been encouraging. A second experiment was on inclusive schooling through the Multi-site Action Research Project involving 23 sites in different states (DIETs, NGO-run schools, private schools, Teachers' College). An Indian adaptation of the UNESCO Teacher Education Resource Pack was used. Again, the experiment generated teacher reflection and problem solving to meet special needs in the classrooms. I am sure many more experiments like this have generated rich experience in the country. The time has come to scale these up, since this experience is lying dormant due to the lack of political will, necessary policy support and the resources to support the regular education system to make education inclusive. This is a critical time for putting the new economic order and human rights issues in the forefront.

Specify Performance Indicators and Monitor the System Reform

I reiterate what I have already said. Let us prepare plans with specific performance indicators. Let us review and enforce accountability for effective implementation at all levels. This is not the enabling condition, but surely a necessary condition for the success of inclusive education.

The Ultimate Goal

The ultimate goal is to ensure quality education for all, including those with special educational needs. When I look for the long term goal, I would like to see 'education' for all. I would like to see that the distinctions between words like 'special education', 'regular education', 'inclusive education' disappear. The practice in these movements will be absorbed in the word 'education'. There will be only education and no special education since it will have the technology to meet the educational needs of all.

References

Government of India (GOI) (1992) *Revised Policy Formulations*, Department of Women and Child, Delhi.

Hegarty, S. (1988) *Review of the Present Situation of Special Education*. Paris: UNESCO.

Jangira, N.K. (1995) 'Rethinking Teacher Education', *Prospects*, XXXV(2): 261–71.

UNESCO (1993) *Teacher Education Resource Package: Special Needs in the Classroom.* Paris: UNESCO.

———— (1994) Final Report of the World Conference on Special Needs Education: Access and Quality at Salamanca, Spain, 10 June 1994. Paris: UNESCO.

4

Teacher Training for Inclusive Education in Developing Countries: The UNESCO Experience

Anupam Ahuja

Tell me, I will forget,
Show me, I may remember,
But involve me and I understand
—A Chinese Proverb

It is now more than 40 years since the nations of the world, speaking through the Universal Declaration of Human Rights, asserted that 'everyone has a right to education'. Yet, it is beyond doubt that across the world many children do not receive adequate education, including large numbers who have disabilities. While in its relatively short existence the field of special education has made much progress, an analysis of the current scene around the world presents a rather disturbing picture. Hegarty (1990: 2) sums up the situation when he states, 'those with disabilities, who ironically have the greatest need of education, are the least likely to receive it. This is true of developed and developing countries alike'. In developed countries many pupils with disabilities and others who fail to achieve satisfactory progress in school learning are formally excluded from the mainstream education system or receive less favourable treatment within it than other children. On the other hand, in many developing countries the continuing struggle to achieve compulsory education for a majority of children takes precedence over meeting the needs of those with disabilities.

How best can we proceed in responding to children who experience difficulties in school, those who have disabilities? Can teachers accommodate pupils with diverse educational needs in the classroom? Are they equipped for accomplishing this task? How should teachers both general and special be trained for teaching in inclusive classrooms? What would be the content and process of such training programmes? For many years the field that is currently known as special educational needs has been alive with disputes on finding the right ways of answering these crucial questions.

In this chapter, the writer describes an important UNESCO initiative that is making a significant contribution towards meeting the needs of children with special needs in ordinary schools. It is seen as part of the overall movement towards 'Education for All'. The efforts using the UNESCO Teacher Education Resource Pack on Special Needs in the Classroom are directed towards preparing teachers in ordinary schools and others in meeting this challenge.

Over the past ten years the writer has been involved with the UNESCO Resource Pack (RP) activities, including the preparation of the pilot version, its tryout, refinement and subsequent extension of ideas, by directing national initiatives in India, Ghana, Nigeria, Sri Lanka, Namibia and Uzbekistan. It is hoped that this account will help readers plan similar initiatives and use it in their contexts for in-service, pre-service and school-based initiatives. The chapter describes the recent movement towards inclusive education and addresses the following questions: How was the UNESCO RP developed? What is its rationale and how is it being used to reinforce community-based rehabilitation programmes (in some cases) as a basis for national, regional and school development initiatives? Examples from several countries are included to draw out what was learned and the challenges faced.

Recent Developments

The world of special educational needs has, it seems, created a problem for itself. For many years it has given the impression that it is a separate field of endeavour, peripheral to the interests of others and largely unconnected to the agenda of the general education community. By thus separating itself from mainstream thinking and practice, it has encouraged a climate that precludes any real consideration of the potential for collaboration between the two sectors. There is an urgent need to bridge this traditional gulf, and all those involved in schooling, whatever their roles, should join together in pooling their energies and resources in order to create schools that can educate all pupils effectively.

An analysis of the development of provision in many Western countries suggests certain patterns (Reynolds and Ainscow, 1994). Provision frequently took the form of separate special schools set up by religious or philanthropic organisations. These were eventually adopted and extended as part of national educational provision, often leading to a separate, parallel school system for those pupils seen as being in need of special arrangements. Similar trends are seen in developing countries (see for example, various chapters in Mittler et al., 1993).

In recent years, the appropriateness of having such separate systems has been challenged both from a human rights perspective (as the title of this conference suggests) and indeed from the point of view of effectiveness. Many research findings relating to this latter point have been reported (Evans, 1993). This has led to an increased emphasis on the notion of integration. Recent international surveys give strong evidence that the integration of pupils said to have special educational needs is seen as being a matter of priority in many countries in both the developed and developing world (see for example Hegarty, 1990; O'Hanlon, 1995).

Research evidence also strongly favours integration. Across many countries, recent reviews of the research literature have demonstrated that disabled children can achieve higher academic standards in integrated settings, although there is also some suggestion that their self-concept may suffer. Integration can take a variety of forms and in itself remains a topic of considerable debate (see for example Norwich, 1990).

Lately, however, we see the emergence of another orientation, that of inclusive schooling. This idea challenges much existing practice in the special needs field. The movement away from traditional views of special education towards inclusive practices has been described as a new paradigm of thought requiring transformation in teacher beliefs and instructional practices (Ballard, 1990; Lipsky and Gartner, 1992; Skrtic, 1991). Indeed, this inclusive orientation is a strong feature of the Salamanca Statement on principles, policy and practice in special needs education agreed by representatives of 92 governments and 25 international organisations in June 1994 (UNESCO, 1994). Specifically, the Statement argues that regular schools with an inclusive orientation are:

> the most effective means of combating discriminatory attitudes, creating welcoming communities, building an inclusive society and achieving education for all; moreover they provide an effective education to the majority of children and improve the efficiency and ultimately the cost effectiveness of the entire education system (pix).

While some critics continue to question the validity and value of inclusion (Fuchs and Fuchs, 1995; Kauffman, 1994; Shanker, 1994), others have focused on what can be learned about effective schools from observing the activities of teachers and students directly involved in the process (Giangreco and Cloninger, 1990; Schnorr, 1990). The reconstruction of teaching approaches, pupil groupings and the use of available support for learning seem to be key features of the inclusion process.

How is inclusive education distinct from integration? The latter usually involves focusing on an individual or small group of pupils for whom the curriculum is adapted with different work devised or support assistants provided. Unlike inclusion, integration does not necessarily challenge or alter in any way the organisation and provision of the curriculum for all pupils. Integration assimilates individual pupils with identified special educational needs into existing forms of schooling. On the other hand, the process of inclusion considers how a school can be restructured in order to respond positively to all pupils as individuals.

Support for the process of inclusion comes from the whole school community and can be of benefit to many pupils, rather than focusing on those pupils who are defined as having special needs. When an inclusive approach is used, specialised services are brought to the child and delivered by support personnel (e.g., teachers, instructional assistants and therapists) in the context of classes (Udavari-Solner, 1993); it is described not as a place or a particular method of instruction, but rather a philosophy of supporting children in their learning, a philosophy that holds that all children can learn (Roach et al., 1995).

As the field of special education internationally continues to seek appropriate ways of moving ahead, a number of writers are adopting a critical perspective, seeking to question theories and assumptions. Examples of writers sharing this perspective include, in Australia, Fulcher (1989); in England, Tomlinson (1982); in New Zealand, Ballard (1990); in Papua New Guinea, Carrier (1983); and in the United States, Skrtic (1991).

One of their concerns is with the way in which pupils within schools come to be designated as having special needs. They see this as a social process that needs to be continually challenged. They argue more specifically that the continued emphasis on explaining educational difficulties in terms of child-centred characteristics has the effect of preventing progress in the field. They all draw on theories from outside special education, such as sociology, politics, philosophy and organisational analysis.

This radical perspective leads to a reconceptualisation of the special needs task (Ainscow, 1991). It suggests the need to consider a general recognition that difficulties experienced by pupils come about as a result of the way schools are artefacts of the traditional curriculum (Skrtic, 1991).

This new perspective on the special needs task is the one that has been adopted and developed in the UNESCO project 'Special Needs in the Classroom'. It is based upon the view that the way forward must be to reform schools in ways that will make them respond positively to pupil diversity, seeking individual differences as something to be nurtured and celebrated. The presumption has been that, within such a conceptualisation, a consideration of the difficulties experienced by pupils and teachers can provide an agenda for reform and indeed insights as to how this might be accomplished.

International Collaboration

In order to develop the Resource Pack, an international network of teachers, teacher educators and administrators was created. The members of this team read draft materials, made suggestions and, in some cases, put forward materials of their own. Following this period of consultation, a pilot version of the Pack was created.

UNESCO ran a workshop and seminar in Zimbabwe for a pair of co-ordinators from eight countries (Canada, Chile, India, Jordan, Kenya, Malta, Spain and Zimbabwe), preparing them to use the Resource Pack. The co-ordinators produced plans for trying the material in initial (pre-service), in-service and school-based training in their own countries.

The style adopted in these trials bore many of the characteristics of action research where participants were encouraged to work in teams using reflective thought, discussion, decision and action in order to develop and refine the thinking and practice of the project. Within this broad orientation, the resource team collected detailed data about their use of pilot materials and produced case studies of their work. They also kept journals in which they made detailed records of their actions, thoughts and feelings, as well as their interpretations of the data they collected.

The data indicated that in all the field-testing sites the materials were used as intended and that course leaders worked in ways that were largely consistent with the thinking associated with the project. The evidence also supports the view that the content of the materials is appropriate for teachers in each of these national contexts, and focuses on issues that they find meaningful and relevant. Furthermore, it seems that the activities and process used are successful in helping both teacher educators and teachers to develop their thinking and practice.

Through systematic analysis of all these data, a series of rationales was developed that could be used to inform the design of the Resource Pack. This entailed providing for the content of the materials, the approaches to teacher education and the strategy for dissemination. As a result of four years of research and development associated with the project the Pack was rewritten. A guide book and video programmes were developed to accompany the Resource Pack.

Subsequently, it has been introduced to groups in over 50 countries and is now the basis of regional development projects in Africa, Asia, Latin America, the Caribbean and Middle East, as well as part of major national initiatives in India, China, Ghana and Thailand. The Pack has been found to be useful in in-service, pre-service and school improvement contexts.

Rationale

The rationale of the UNESCO project is to encourage the development of mainstream classroom practices that can take account of the needs of all children as individuals. It can be seen as part of the overall movement towards 'Education for All' whilst at the same time encouraging the creation of inclusive schooling as recommended by the Salamanca State-ment and Framework for Action on special needs in education.

The main focus is on making effective use of resources, particular-ly through collaboration between teachers, pupils, parents and the wider community. Such moves are seen as contributing to the overall effectiveness of the school system. Use is made of teacher education processes that encourage learning from experience through personal reflection and co-operation between colleagues. These processes are demonstrated during participatory workshop sessions based upon materials in the Resource Pack. The participants are encouraged to plan work with colleagues in their workplaces to support implementation of new teaching responses. These two ideas, reflection and collaboration, are at the heart of the approaches being used within the UNESCO project.

Our experience of using approaches based upon these ideas in many different countries suggests that they can be influential in encouraging teacher educators and teachers to see improvement as a fundamental area of their work. We have also found that these ways of working can encourage teachers to adopt a more flexible view of difficulties experienced by pupils in their classes, a view that sees such difficulties as a source of feedback on existing classroom arrangements. Indeed, this feedback provides information as to how classroom arrangements can be improved in ways that are beneficial to the whole class. As a result, in responding to the experience and existing knowledge of individual pupils, schools improve.

Our attempts to introduce teacher educators and teachers to these two strategies are based upon five sets of approaches that have been developed and refined within the project. These are as follows:

1. Active learning: Approaches such as co-operative group work that encourage participants to engage with opportunities for learning.
2. Negotiation of objectives: Approaches that enable teacher development activities to take account of the concerns and interests of individual participants.
3. Demonstration, practice and feedback: Approaches that model examples of practice, encourage their use in the classroom and incorporate opportunities for supportive feedback.
4. Continuous evaluation: Approaches that encourage enquiry and reflection as ways of reviewing learning.
5. Support: Approaches that help individuals to take risks.

Teams in many countries are now using the UNESCO Resource Pack as part of their teacher education activities. As they do so, they are involved in further research that will contribute to the continuous refinement and expansion of the ideas included in the material.

National Developments

Having traced the movement towards inclusive education and seen how the UNESCO Pack has developed and its rationale, let us look at some national contexts.

India

The last decade has been significant for educational developments in India. Previously, the range of provision for children with special needs varied from exclusion, through minimal provision, to limited coverage in special or regular schools. The health and social welfare systems were also inadequately developed.

Lately, however, it has been realised that inclusive schooling is not an alternative choice but an inevitability, if the dream of providing quality basic education to all children is to ever become a reality. This necessitates teacher education reform to be developed within India's unique socio-cultural and economic contexts. Theoretically sound and practically feasible teacher development programmes are our goal.

Of the many initiatives taken towards meeting the needs of all children in the general school system, the UNICEF-assisted PIED, begun in 1986, was seen as a significant breakthrough. However, we also became aware of several limitations. Despite an emphasis on integration, we found that categorisation, labelling and exclusion from educational activities continued. We also noticed that more schoolchildren were being identified as having special needs. Were schools identifying more marginal children as pupils with special needs in order to take advantage of additional funding? Also, despite our effort to make the training of teachers learner-centred, the didactic component of teacher training continued to be on the high side. In our minds questions were also arising about the cost effectiveness of the three-level teacher training programme, given the number of teachers involved and the resources.

At this juncture (in mid-1989), a senior colleague and the writer were invited to act as co-ordinators of the advisory team to review and select materials for the UNESCO project. The philosophy and approach seemed to be relevant to the issues arising out of our review of PIED.

The draft UNESCO pack was ready in early 1990. We learned to transact the approach in different teacher education contexts at a workshop and seminar held in Zimbabwe in 1990. We planned to use it in India in pre-service and in-service contexts, suggest modifications and new materials, and develop video programmes.

The field test was done in an in-service situation and in a pre-service context. The testing was spread over a period of 11 weeks. The gaps between training periods were utilised by the teachers to incorporate learning and teaching activities in their classrooms. The pre-service teachers also used the knowledge in their practice teaching. Overall, the field testing indicated a positive change in teachers' attitudes, classroom climate and school atmosphere.

All this experience, as well as our learning from other friends engaged in similar exercises across the globe, was summarised in a subregional workshop and seminar for Asia held in November 1991.

Following these earlier experiences, a national project was designed known as the 'Multi-site Action Research Project' (MARP). It provides examples of functional networking for change. Besides preparation of vertical and horizontal networking, the project experimented with the institutionalisation of innovative change.

Encouraging teacher training institutions at primary and secondary levels and schools to join was one of the major objectives of MARP. Out of 40 institutions approached, 22 participated. The project involved 33 co-ordinators from 22 institutions (nine district institutes of education and training, eight colleges of education and university departments, three schools and NGOs). Two individuals from each institution were selected to encourage collaboration and mutual support at workshops. Training and practice in the use of the UNESCO Pack were provided, based on the experience gathered. Action research projects were developed in pre-service, in-service and school-based contexts.

The various projects followed a pre-test/post-test, single group design. Pupils and students were selected randomly. Participants were required to document the process and provide data with examples. The project involved 338 experienced teachers, 248 pre-service teachers and 9,986 children in 115 schools spread over 23 sites in different parts of the country. The project has become part of institutional practice.

The project sites have become resource centres for further extension of the project in neighbouring schools. It exemplifies the networking of teacher training institutions, school clusters, individual schools and non-government agencies working with teachers as well as local education authorities. It has widely influenced policy formulation for training in-service and pre-service teachers as a component of educational reform in our country. In addition, the methodology has been included by policy makers and planners in various national teacher education programmes. In Uttar Pradesh, the master trainers under the UP Education for All projects have been trained using these approaches.

Expanding the experiment to reach out to a large number of schools under DPEPs is planned. It is a big step towards the institutionalisation of systematic change. In-service training of teachers is being viewed as crucial to its success.

These experiences demonstrate that in-service and pre-service training require teaching skills for teachers and those who provide support to them. It involves changes in thinking and practice to bring about systematic change and to organise effective schools for all children. It includes reflection and problem-solving skills for professional development. Everyone needs to be involved. Training should be continuous, relevant and as close to the workplace situation as possible. Provision for demonstration, practice and feedback to ensure mastery over knowledge and skills in the context of the workplace is essential. Individuals should be encouraged to plan action research to transfer and fine-tune new skills according to demands. It is essential to explore, plan and support collaboration in the workplace as an integral component of the training design to ensure the transfer of knowledge and skills and institutionalise the change. Our experience in India indicates that school-based in-service training programmes encouraging a whole-school approach help to bring about systematic change and can be an effective strategy.

Namibia

Formerly known as South West Africa, Namibia gained its independence in 1991 after an arduous liberation struggle. There has been rapid expansion of the education system since that date, with high levels of government expenditure on education in an endeavour to improve access to and the quality of education for all citizens (for example, 35 per cent of the national budget in 1994–95).

Along with dismantling the previous tripartite education systems for white, coloured and black citizens, reforms have included the introduction of English as the medium of instruction for classes above Grade 4, replacing of Afrikaans, and the establishment of a Directorate of Special Education and Culture. Other directorates govern teacher training (National Institute of Educational Development, NIED) and curriculum development (Educational Programmes Implementation, EPID).

There are seven education regions, but resources tend to be concentrated in the region round the capital, Windhoek, where, for example, the teacher/pupil ratio is 1 to 22 or 23, contrasted with 1 to 38 in the Ondangwa region (1992 figures). Each region has a Directorate of Education and a staff of school inspectors who monitor mainstream education, and school counsellors who are responsible for special educational needs in special schools. In the mainstream, special education provision is limited, despite efforts to expand facilities since 1991. There are six special schools, four of which are in Windhoek, and a programme of expansion which centres on the training of remedial teachers for mainstream schools.

A large inter-agency project, with NAD as a co-operating agency, is developing a community-based rehabilitation programme in Namibia. Promoting inclusive education within the project in the next two years was the subject of a plan worked out by the Ministry of Education and UNESCO and the technical input needed to be identified. To begin the task, an exercise was carried out to mobilise interest, support and commitment of schools to participate in the project. Advice and assistance to the national counterparts were provided in carrying out the preparatory tasks.

A mission was undertaken in October 1996 to support the implementation of inclusive education policies within the CBR project using the Pack. Separate tasks were carried out in a sequence of varying periods of time, each targeting a distinct group and discriminating between conference, orientation and intensive training for the special audiences.

The participants were very positive about the ideas and techniques to which they were introduced. All the groups moved from scepticism about inclusive education to a more hopeful and realistic grasp of its implications in their own educational context. Certainly the profile of inclusive education as the most appropriate strategy for meeting special needs in the classroom has been highlighted. Teachers, administrators and others who attended the events planned national initiatives to promote the ideas so that the momentum was not lost.

Sri Lanka

In Sri Lanka, not too long ago, only a few selected children with special needs benefited from the existing system of special institutions. The vast majority remained in their homes without any opportunity for education or social adjustment. The situation underwent a major change in 1971 with the establishment of a Special Education Unit at the Ministry of Education. For the first time, the government undertook direct respons- ibility for providing educational opportunities for handicapped children. Significant progress in the provision of educational opportunities was made during the 1970s with the number of special schools increasing to 21. During the same time, the concept of integrating disabled children into the mainstream also gathered momentum in the Sri Lankan educational system. Implementation of the policy gained ground year by year. At the request of state departments, such as the Social Services Department and Probation Department, the policy of integration has received accept- ance from the community although the innovation was brought about by professionals. The main obstacle to the nation-wide expansion of special education is the non-availability of trained personnel in the field.

In the early 1990s, a strong need was felt to develop appropriate teacher training materials, which could assist teacher trainers in different training programmes. It was thought that such material could contribute to uniformity and quality in short and long term in-service and pre-service training programmes. The aim was to upgrade the pedagogical skills of teachers with a focus on greater interaction between the teachers and the pupils as well as among the pupils. The National Institute of Education, Colombo took up the task of developing a uniform Basic Teacher Training Manual.

In line with the need and with national developments, it was decided to base the manual on the UNESCO Teacher Resource Pack. To start off, the Pack was translated into Sinhala and later into Tamil. A two-week workshop based on the Pack was organised for a group. Fifty-two teacher educators were carefully selected to include members from the NIE Department (post-graduate teacher education), government training colleges, and primary school teachers. During the workshop, innovative teaching methods to promote effective learning for all students in the classroom were explored. Brief presentations were also made on the Esculla Nueva experiences in Colombia, and on topics of national interest such as teachers' problems in Sri Lanka and teaching children in rural schools.

This exercise was followed by field testing the translated version of the Pack at teacher colleges, pre-service colleges of education, distance education centres and some schools. The results indicate appropriateness of the approaches in the varied contexts with an emphasis on co-operative learning to bring about changes in the strategies and methods of teacher education. The focus was on learning more than teaching. The Resource Pack is being introduced in the colleges of education (pre-service) to include it as an integral part of teacher education curriculum.

Ghana

Ghana, a small country on the west coast in Sub-Saharan Africa, is predominantly a rural society. There are approximately one million disabled people out of a population of 16.9 million (UNICEF, 1996). Based on a WHO estimate made for several developing countries, the prevalence of disabled people in Ghana is 5 to 7 per cent. This percentage is lower than the 10 per cent usually found in industrialised countries because the elderly are so few. Also the disabled have a much higher mortality rate and this reduces quite considerably the prevalence of disability. The under-five mortality rate is 131, and 27 per cent of the children are underweight and the same percentage under the age of 3 years are malnourished (ibid.). All these are at-risk children. The situation becomes even more complicated since the existing services can do no more than scratch the surface of providing for the needs.

Various estimates within Ghana state that no more than 2 per cent of children with special needs are getting any form of service (Ofori Addo, 1993). One of the key obstacles to the integration of disabled children in the regular school system is the geographical distance between community and schools. Distances as great as 5 km between communities and the nearest school prevent children with special needs from attending them. In addition to this, the existing school facilities are extremely inadequate.

In September 1987, the Government of Ghana embarked upon a new educational reform programme to improve both access and the quality of education. Special education was to be administered as part of the general education system and follow the ordinary curriculum with modifications as required.

A peripatetic service was created to reach greater numbers. Carrying out a very traditional task of only identifying disabled children and recommending their placement in special schools, a peripatetic teacher was sometimes covering 30 schools or more depending on the district. A need was being felt to provide additional inputs to help peripatetic teachers fulfil their role better. In an attempt to broaden the skills and vision of these teachers and prepare them to continue experimenting and searching for context-specific solutions, training based on the UNESCO Resource Pack was suggested.

Various initiatives with the Pack involving different actors (including peripatetic teachers) were developed progressively with the CBR programme. These have greatly reinforced the CBR programme and have had a significant impact on the implementation of the education policy promoting the philosophy and practice of inclusive schooling. Through regional training activities the focus has been to help peripatetic teachers (with special needs skills), ordinary school teachers, headteachers, teacher educators, district level administrators, regional co-ordinators and the CBR manager to respond to children with special education needs in regular local schools. A national core team was formed to give an impetus to the national dissemination and training activities, and to establish good practice in schools.

During the various workshops and seminars, participants became more confident and skilful in their ability to cater for pupil diversity in the classroom. They were encouraged to use the resources of others around them, including the pupils. Opportunities were provided for constant reflection and review of their new knowledge and skills in the context of practices in the workplace. The use of co-operative learning approaches was encouraged and means of utilising existing resources for the purpose of problem solving in educational contexts explored. All the sessions were greeted with interest and enthusiasm by participants. They felt that the approaches and materials were relevant and feasible in the Ghanaian context. However, difficulties were anticipated because of limited resources.

Keeping these in mind, the conditions and resources available during the workshops were intentionally planned to be as close to the workplace situation as possible. In Ajumako, half the workshop room had piled up extra furniture, poor flooring, bad lighting and acoustics. In addition to these conditions, in Sommanya sights, such as stray ducks and hens strolling into the room, were common. The disadvantage of limited resources including workshop materials was converted into a challenge and an opportunity to find out alternative low cost indigenous material.

Very often, when the required stationery items to run the workshop were not available we demonstrated how we could improvise. In place of ordinary flip charts (for compiling group reactions, poster making, etc.), lightweight thin paper was often joined together to get the required size. It was provided a thicker base by sticking old newspapers. Crayons and charcoal, refilled sketch pens, etc., were often used as writing material. Local crude home-made glue replaced the Scotch tape. Instead of thumb pins, needle and thread were used to stitch the flip charts on dried grass mats. The blackboard was also used to collate ideas. In one instance, participants used the floor to write with chalk their compiled list of thoughts. Having got the message, they wanted to demonstrate how one can work in situations where there is not even a blackboard available!

During some workshops, the much needed pin boards were not available to put up flip charts with salient messages that the groups prepared. Instead excellent improvised display boards made out of local lightweight wood were used. Grass mats and dried coconut leaves hung between wooden frames were also used. These frames had movable bolts, which helped to hold and adjust the length of the mats, etc. Flip charts were stitched on these mats/leaves.

One of the most fundamental realisations was that one could work even with very limited materials. This was evident not just in the workshop sessions but also in the schools where the participants carried out the follow-up exercises. The group realised that all material limitations can be compensated for if the participants are zealous and are actively involved.

What Have We Learned?

Our experience of setting up initiatives based upon the Pack in a range of countries indicates that the experiences have made a significant impact on the overall quality of schools. At the same time, however, participants must be prepared for periods of turbulence which are inevitable features of attempts to innovate in educational contexts. The nature of this phenomenon varies from place to place, but ideas and approaches that disrupt the status quo of their day-to-day lives can be challenging. In the light of these possible difficulties it is vital to create a strong infrastructure of teamwork so that individuals can support one another in dealing with the inevitable pressure of leading the process of change. It is also important that freedom is allowed for modification and flexible use in order to accommodate circumstances in particular contexts.

While transacting the various workshops and seminars, having a philosophy of not forcing or expecting any overnight change proved extremely beneficial for all. Experience tells us that in terms of both particular classroom culture and, more critically, particular personal histories and teacher attitudes, teacher change can be a very personal matter. They may be reluctant to give up ways of working that have proved helpful on earlier occasions. We constantly reminded ourselves that the best way to introduce innovations in schools was to create conditions and contexts that enable teachers to work at their own pace, experimenting and exploring their own change process. Work in various countries also indicates that change for teachers does not always happen in the ways 'experts' describe it because the realities of teaching are different from idealised versions. While introducing the group to new ways, care was taken to ensure that no one felt discredited or criticised because of their earlier practice.

From the experiences in this particular UNESCO project we have noted the following key strategies that facilitate the implementation of innovations:

Flexible Use of Adaptable Materials

The rationale of the project has led to the preparation of teacher education materials that are intended to encourage reflection and collaboration. Consequently, the materials are designed in such a way as to include short pieces of text that will stimulate course participants to draw on their own experience and knowledge. Course sessions focus on agendas related to workplace concerns and address problems faced by teachers in their classrooms. Participants had opportunities to experience a variety of active learning approaches. Teachers were encouraged to consider life in the classroom through the eyes of their own practice in schools. It is also vital that the content of the materials is based upon well-developed principles and a cohesive rationale.

Preparation of Personnel

An important key to successful project implementation is the careful preparation of those personnel who will be asked to adopt co-ordinating responsibilities. Within the UNESCO project, small teams of co-ordinators were created in particular settings (for example, in a college or a school). They were introduced to the thinking and practice of the project through demonstrations, explanations of theory, practice and feedback. Members of the teams then collaborated in the implementation process at their workplace, using the notion of peer coaching where partners assisted one another to experiment with new approaches.

Local Decision Making

In order that local circumstances and needs can be accommodated, it is helpful for planning decisions to be made by those near to 'the action'. Consequently, within the project, co-ordinators were asked to take responsibility for formulating their own action plans. Appropriate adaptations are made to the materials and, at the same time, co-ordinators develop a commitment to the success of their initiative. Loyalty amongst members of the team further contributes to this sense of responsibility for what occurs. We have found that using action research is a powerful means of encouraging these developments.

Support at All Levels

Involvement in innovative projects can sometimes be stressful, particularly during the early days when there is a strong possibility of turbulence. Consequently, the implementation strategy must place particular emphasis on the establishment of a support system for key individuals. Of course, the creation of co-ordinator teams is an important factor here, but we have found it helpful to encourage people to think strategically about other possible sources of support. It is particularly critical to ensure the goodwill of important individuals and agencies within the community so that, at the very least, their active opposition is prevented. The establishment of networks of communication, both formal and informal, is an important means of encouraging a feeling of involvement in project activities.

Challenges

The innovations in using the Pack have been successful, though the pace and quality could have improved with better environment conditions. In carrying through the innovations to meet special needs in the classroom there have been problems typical of many developing countries. Initially, substantial time and effort were required to change the attitudes of administrators, build partnerships and facilitate a convergence of effort.

Limited resources, crowded classes, inadequate furniture, examination-oriented curricula, etc., placed demands on teachers which initially discouraged them from the innovation and from trying to meet the needs of every child in the class. Lack of financial support for the innovation also caused impediments of its own kind, till experience proved change is possible even with limited resources. All the UNESCO initiatives relied solely on one-shot training sessions. The possibility of using a simultaneous training transfer model could not be explored because of time constraints. However, involving varied professionals, such as ordinary school teachers, peripatetic teachers, headteachers, teacher educators, special educators, CBR managers and administrators proved very beneficial.

Final Reflections

At the outset of the UNESCO project, a number of colleagues suggested that the idea of a single resource pack that could be used in many countries was impossible. Their concern was that contextual and cultural factors would make the content of such a pack unsuitable in many countries. In some senses, of course, these colleagues are correct. If we were to develop a pack requiring the rigid acceptance of specific content, it would only be relevant to a limited extent. The Resource Pack is therefore used to stimulate the creation of appropriate responses to specific situations rather than to encourage the adoption of ready-made prescriptions imported from elsewhere.

This is arguably the most significant outcome of the research associated with the project. We have learned that improvements in teacher education are most likely to occur when groups of people collaborate to explore their experiences and understanding. This often inspires creativity and innovation.

Therefore, those wishing to develop innovative projects in education must remember the important message that people matter most. The best strategy is to create networks of colleagues who are encouraged to collaborate in making the innovation succeed. They may draw on ideas and materials from elsewhere, but the basis for improvement is their own combined efforts. In our view, the message applies equally to regional, national and school-based initiatives.

References

Ainscow, M. (ed.) (1991) *Effective Schools for All*. London: Fulton.

——— (1993a) 'Teacher Education as Strategy for Developing Inclusive Schools', in R. Slee (ed.) *Is There a Desk with My Name on it? The Politics of Integration*. London: Falmer.

——— (1993b) 'Beyond Special Education: Some Ways Forward', in J. Visser and G. Upton (eds) *Special Education in Britain after Warnock*. London: Fulton.

Ainscow, M. (1993c) 'Teacher Education and Special Needs: Some Lessons from the UNESCO Project'. 'Special needs in the classroom', in P. Mittler et al. (eds) *Special Needs Education* (World Yearbook). London: Kegan Paul.

———— (1994a) Special Needs in the Classroom: A Teacher Education Guide. London: Jessica Kingsley/UNESCO.

———— (1994b) 'Supporting International Innovation in Teacher Education', in H.W. Bradley, et al. (eds) *Developing Teachers, Developing Schools*. London: Fulton.

Ainscow, M., N.K. Jangira and **A. Ahuja** (1995) 'Responding to Special Needs through Teacher Development', in P. Zinkin and H. McConachie (eds) Disabled Children and Developing Countries. London: Mackeith Press.

Ballard, K.D. (1990) 'Special Education in New Zealand: Disability, Politics and Empowerment', International Journal of Disability, Development and Education, 37(2): 109–24.

Carrier, J.G. (1983) 'Masking the Social in Educational Knowledge: The Case of Learning Disability Theory', *American Journal of Sociology*, 88, 948–74.

Evans, P. (ed.) (1993) *European Journal of Special Needs Education*. Special Edition on Integration, 8(3).

Fuchs, D. and **L.S. Fuchs** (1995) 'Sometimes Separate is Better', *Educational Leadership*, (52): 22–24.

Fulcher, G. (1989) *Disabling Policies? A Comparative Approach to Education Policy and Disability*. London: Falmer.

Giangreco, M.F. and **C.J. Cloninger** (1990). 'Facilitating Inclusion through Problem Solving Methods', *TASH Newsletter*, 16(5): 10.

Hegarty, S. (1981) 'Philosophical Basis for a New Paradigm', in P. Reason and J. Rowan (eds) *Human Inquiry*. Chichester: Wiley.

———— (1990) *The Education of Children and Young People with Disabilities: Principals and Practice*. Paris: UNESCO.

Jangira, N.K. and **A. Ahuja** (1992) *Effective Teacher Training Co-operative Learning Based Approach*. New Delhi: National Publishing House.

Kauffman, J. (1994) 'How We Might Achieve the Radical Reform of Special Education', *Exceptional Children*, 60: 6–16.

Lipsky, D. and **A. Gartner** (1989) *Beyond Separate Education. Quality Education for All*. Balimora: Paul H. Brookes.

———— (1992) 'Achieving Full Inclusion: Placing the Student at the Centre of Educational Reform', in W. Stainback and S. Stainback (eds) *Controversial Issue Confronting Special Education: Divergent Perspectives*. Needham Heights, MA: Allyn and Bacon.

Mittler, P., R. Brouillette and **D. Harris** (eds) (1993) *Special Education* (World Yearbook of Education). London: Kegan Paul.

Norwich, B. (1990) Reappraising Special Needs Education. London: Cassell.

Ofori Addo, L. (1993) *The CBR Programmes in Ghana: Examples of Good Practice in Special Needs Education and CBR Programmes*. Paris: UNESCO.

O'Hanlon C. (ed.) (1995) *Inclusive Education in Europe*. London: Fulton.

Reynolds, M.C. and **M. Ainscow** (1994) 'Education of Children and Youth with Special Needs: An International Perspective', in T. Husen and T. Postlethwaite (eds) *The International Encyclopaedia of Education*, Second edn. Oxford: Blackwell.

Virginia, R., J. Ascroft and **A. Stamp** (1995) *Winning Ways: Creating Inclusive Schools, Classrooms, and Communities*. Alexandria, V.A.: National Association of State Boards of Education.

Salisbury, C., M.M. Palombaro and **T. Hollowood** (1993) 'On the Nature of Change in an Inclusive Elementary School, *Journal of the Association for Persons with Severe Handicaps*, 18: 75–84.

Schnorr, R. (1990) 'Peter? He Comes and Goes': First Grades' Perspectives on a Part-Time Mainstream Student', *Journal of the Association for Persons with Severe Handicaps*, 15: 231–40.

Shanker, A. (1994) 'Where We Stand: Inclusion and Ideology', *The New York Times*, 6 February, p. 7.

Skrtic, T.M. (1991) 'Students with Special Educational Needs: Artifacts of the Traditional Curriculum', in M. Ainscow (ed.) *Effective Schools for All*. London: Fulton.

Slavin, R.E. (1995) *Co-operative Learning: Theory Research Practice*, Second edn. Boston: Allyn & Bacon.

Tomlinson, S. (1982) *A Sociology of Special Education*. London: Routledge.

Udavari-Solner, A. ([1988] 1993) 'Inclusive Education', in C. Grant and G. Landson Billings (eds) *The Dictionary of Multicultural Education*. Paris: UNESCO.

UNESCO (1994) *The Salamanca Statement and Framework on Special Needs Education*. Paris: UNESCO.

——— (1988) *Review of the Present Situation in Special Education*. Paris: UNESCO.

——— (1993) *Teacher Education Resource Pack on Special Needs in the Classroom*. Paris: UNESCO.

UNICEF (1996) *The Progress of Nations 1996*. New York: UNICEF. pp. 19–29, 36, 52.

5

Integrated Education for Disabled Children: Cost Effective Approaches

M.N.G. Mani

The last one and a half decades have witnessed a phenomenal growth of integrated education for disabled children in India. Integrated education was initially conceptualised as an alternative approach to bring all those unreached disabled children under the umbrella of education. It was projected by governments and voluntary agencies as the economically viable, psychologically superior, and socially accepted model for the education of disabled children, *but the ground level realities indicate that the progress made so far is not satisfactory.* Statistics reveal that not even 5 per cent of disabled children in India have been served even after the implementation of an integrated system of education since 1975. At this pace, another 3 to 4 decades may be necessary to serve all disabled children, and further incidence of disability may also make the target far to reach. At such a slow pace, statistics and projections may remain mere intellectual exercises.

Existing Models of Integrated Education

In any policy there are two equally important factors—conceptualisation and execution. In India, conceptual clarity on integrated education is found among organisations working for disabled persons and professionals as well. There is consensus that integrated education should aim at normalising the life and education of the disabled child, but opinions vary to a great extent in realising the goal of integration. A minimum of ten implementing strategies of integrated education are currently observed in India:

1. Resource model where disabled children study in general schools and stay in hostels meant for non-disabled children.
2. Resource model where disabled children study in general schools and stay in hostels of the nearby special schools.
3. Resource model where disabled children study in general schools and stay in hostels exclusively created for them.
4. Resource model where disabled children study in general schools and stay with parents at home.
5. Semi-resource model or cooperative model where disabled children are taught only by the resource teacher in a separate class in a general school.
6. Itinerant plan where a resource teacher visits the child in his/her local school and the child stays with parents.
7. Multi-category resource plan where disabled children of different kinds are educated in a general school by the regular teachers and a specialist teacher.
8. Multi-category itinerant plan where one special teacher attends to the needs of disabled children of different categories in a particular locality.
9. Dual-teacher plan where a general classroom teacher assumes responsibility for education of one or two disabled children of his/her class with minimal training.
10. Composite area approach where at least one teacher from every school is supposed to have short-term training in the area of special education and all teachers in the school receive a week-long orientation in dealing with disabled children. The teachers and children in this programme are assisted by specialists as well as multi-skilled teachers.

Resource models with residential facilities are predominantly found in Tamil Nadu. Resource models with non-residential facilities are found in Orissa and Madhya Pradesh. Itinerant programmes are mostly found in Gujarat and Maharashtra. Multi-category approaches are found in

Rajasthan, Haryana, and many specific projects in different states. The dual-teacher plan is found in Mizoram and Nagaland where transportation between different localities is inadequate. The composite area approach is in practice in the PIED supported by UNICEF in ten representative blocks in the country.

There are claims and counter claims in the country about the superiority of one model over the other. In this professional debate on models, the real thrust of integrated education is being missed.

In deciding the cost effective models of integrated education, three factors have to be considered:

- availability of disabled children in a locality,
- nature of services required by disabled children, and
- expertise needed for a special teacher and general classroom teachers.

Disabled Children—Found Mostly in Rural Areas

More than 95 per cent of disabled children in the country, especially those in the rural areas, are scattered. In a rural locality, it is difficult to find out the required number of disabled children of a particular category to justify the starting of a resource model. There may be three visually impaired, two hearing impaired and two mentally retarded children, and therefore, a resource model, if started, may become expensive. In such circumstances, the only cost effective model would be a multi-category approach where one resource teacher can attend to the needs of all disabled children with the assistance of general classroom teachers. Research clearly indicates that the resource model is academically superior to all other models of integration but duplication of the resource model for mass implementation is not feasible. Wherever disabled children of a particular category are available in adequate number, starting a resource model is appropriate with a clear-cut understanding that the approach may have to be flexible when the enrolment pattern changes in the course of time. The common scene today is that the resource model once started is not changed, even after all children of that particular locality are fully served. In order to justify the continuance of the resource model, disabled children from far off places are brought to the programme by creating hostel facilities or using the existing hostels meant for non-disabled children. This approach defeats the very fundamental concept of integrated education, and such an education becomes as costly as a special school setting.

Therefore, implementing agencies should fix short term as well as long term goals in programme implementation and also be ready to change approaches when the backlog of disabled children is cleared. The national policies suggest both multi-category and single category models for implementation. Both can function within a plan of an implementing agency. Unless this flexibility is acknowledged, services for disabled children will not expand as expected. A multi-category model, in most cases, is not an option but certainly an inevitable strategy for multiplying the services for disabled children.

Nature of Services Required by Disabled Children

Data from the PIED evaluation study indicate that disabled children ranging from mild to severe categories can be classified as per the nature of educational assistance required by them. The classifications are as follows:

- Category 1 includes children with mild disabilities who can be handled by general classroom teachers with a sensitisation training of one week. Around 45 per cent of the disabled children belong to this category.
- Category 2 includes children with mild/moderate disabilities who need counselling services from time to time. These children can also be handled by regular classroom teachers with minimal training not exceeding two weeks. Around 30 per cent of disabled children come under this category.
- Category 3 includes children with moderate/severe disabilities who need resource assistance, including corrective aids, and periodical help in academic areas. General classroom teachers who are given a crash course of three months' duration can perform this role effectively. Around 15 per cent of disabled children can be classified under this category.
- Category 4 includes children with severe disabilities who require direct attention/preparatory assistance from special teachers.

A multi-category teacher or a single speciality teacher may be required for this category of disabled children. Only 10 per cent of disabled children come under this category.

Therefore, all levels of disabled children can be served effectively by a good combination of specialists, multi-category teachers and general classroom teachers. Use of general classroom teachers is a vital factor for providing education for all disabled children. Special education programmes working in isolation cannot make the EFA a reality. The majority of the disabled children can be handled by general classroom teachers and, therefore, the dual-teaching approach (teaching both disabled and non-disabled children in the general classroom by the classroom teacher) has vast potential. The nature of training, teaching responsibilities, etc., have to be worked out for the smooth implementation of this approach.

Need for Single Category as well as Multi-Category Teachers

The evaluation of PIED undertaken by UNICEF projects a need for 50,000 resource teachers in India to serve all disabled children up to middle school level. The composition of specialists recommended is as follows:

Teachers of Visually Impaired (10%)	⟶	5,000
Teachers of Hearing Impaired (10%)	⟶	5,000
Teachers of Mentally Retarded (10%)	⟶	5,000
Specialists in Orthopaedic Handicap (10%)	⟶	5,000
Multi-category Teachers (60%)	⟶	30,000

These figures acknowledge the need for both single speciality teachers as well as multi-category teachers. Therefore, there is no need for apprehension about multi-category programmes. These two approaches should go hand-in-hand so that a good combination of specialists and multi-category teachers can be prepared to serve all disabled children, varying from mild to severe disabilities. The existing multi-category training centres are far from adequate and, therefore, expansion of similar programmes becomes vital.

Three-tier System of General Education: The Caveats in Replication

General education follows a three-tier system in teacher recruitment. A primary level teacher is just a matriculate with two years of training in teaching methods, while two bachelors' degrees—one in a subject area and another in education—are essential for recruitment as a secondary level teacher. For higher secondary level, the teacher should be a subject specialist with a post-graduate degree in the particular discipline.

Can this System be Replicated in Services for Disabled Children?

The system is applicable in a special school setting, but it becomes expensive in an integrated setting. In integrated education, the disabled children are distributed in different classes. Suppose there are ten disabled children in an integrated school—three at the primary level, four at the secondary level and three at the higher secondary level. Is it possible to have three resource teachers? Literature clearly recommends that a resource teacher should be allowed to serve disabled children cutting across all levels.

In a government setting, a primary level teacher is considered to be less qualified for handling higher classes. This recruitment pattern needs to be relaxed in the case of integrated education. A resource teacher should preferably be a graduate teacher, irrespective of the school where s/he is working and be allowed to work with disabled children cutting across all levels. There may be occasional personality issues that the resource teacher is the most qualified person in a primary school or even draws more pay than the head of the school, but this risk is better than simply replicating a three-tier model which may be more expensive in the long run. This flexibility in teacher recruitment is vital for the expansion of services for disabled children at a price the governments can afford.

Optimistic Hypotheses

In India, all approaches of integrated education are working. What is required is the acceleration of the services. The real acceleration will happen only when

- education of disabled children becomes the responsibility of states;
- education of disabled children, whether in special schools or integrated schools, comes under the Department of Education;
- single category and multi-category teachers work hand-in-hand by shedding the rivalry between them;
- special schools are equipped further to meet the needs of multiply disabled children;
- the general education system is sensitised to the needs of special needs children; and
- general classroom teachers are equipped to serve mildly and moderately disabled children.

In India, special education institutions are working in isolation. There is very little co-ordination between service providers. Resources between organisations are seldom exchanged. In the debate on quality and quantity of service programmes, the disabled child should not become a victim. It is necessary to strike a balance between quality and quantity so that the presently unreached disabled children can get a taste of educational services. All organisations—both government supported and private bodies—have to be brought together, for providing comprehensive services to disabled children by adopting cost effective approaches of integrated education.

6

Integrating Disability Concerns in Primary Education: The Maharasthra Experience

Madhuri Pai[1]

Introduction and Background

Education for all by 2000 AD is the objective of the Government of India. Several steps are being taken to improve enrolments, contain dropout rates, increase sustainability and provide opportunities for non-formal education as well as adult education. The World Bank co-sponsored project on universalisation of primary education—UPE envisages inclusion of all children in the school system. Consequently, the implementation agency, DPEP, also has a mandate for including children with special needs in primary schools.

Although appropriate policies, resources and attitudes for integrating disabled children in primary schools exist in DPEP, it lacks necessary expertise in identification of specific needs, intervention techniques and follow-up systems. The Spastic Society of India (SSI), known for its quality service, innovative approach and commitment to disabled children, possesses the right experience, trained manpower and necessary professional network for bringing all children under the umbrella of education. However, it lacks the infrastructure and financial resources necessary for decentralisation of services. The current project was initiated with the hope that this gap between resources and service delivery could be bridged with an active collaboration between DPEP and SSI.

Dimension of the Problem

Statistics on the number of disabled children under the age of six in India vary widely. Surveys are very patchy and stratification criteria for disability are not defined clearly. Naturally, identification is very difficult. According to the GOI data, of the 12 per cent of the population under 14 years of age, only 4.3 per cent had completed their primary education from the formal school system. Similar data for disabled children are not available.

It is estimated that over 90 per cent of India's 15 million severely disabled young children live in rural areas in conditions of extreme poverty and poor health. Faulty dietary habits, lack of information on prevention and poor access to medical facilities continue to increase the population of disabled children in the country. Against the backdrop of this social setting, it is not surprising that less that 1 per cent of children with special needs have access to professional intervention, especially education. Furthermore, statistics also show that special education is at least 20 times as expensive as regular education and since the government relies heavily on the voluntary sector for special education and rehabilitation, these services have hardly touched rural India. Children with special needs from rural areas are therefore left out of the education system.

In Maharashtra state, DPEP was introduced four years ago. Site selection was based on the data provided by the State Council of Educational Research and Training. At present, five districts 450 km from Mumbai have been chosen for implementation of UPE strategies. These districts were chosen because they were found to have the lowest literacy rates and highest school dropout rates in the state. A detailed plan for building new schools, providing equipment and manpower training was developed. Unfortunately, disability issues were not considered till November 1996, when SSI collaboration was initiated.

Issues Addressed

The current study is to be carried out in three phases:

- Obtain baseline data on disability in selected small areas called clusters. A comparison with the secondary data obtained from the health offices at the taluka levels will be carried out.

- Educate the education officers, teachers and headmasters of DPEP schools about the need for inclusion and importance of integrated education. Implications of inclusive education policy alternative will also be discussed with them.
- As a pilot intervention model, a small group of mild to moderately disabled children will be mainstreamed in a suitable neighbourhood school.

It is envisaged that SSI will use its expertise to monitor the placement and progress of these children. Teachers concerned will be given a brief training in intervention strategies.

While this pilot project is being implemented, using the local network of health officers, data on disability will be collected from all villages under the jurisdiction of DPEP. A plan for integrating all children in the district will be worked out only after such data become available.

It is hoped that the results from the pilot project will provide guidelines for the training programme for all teachers in primary schools. Preference will be given to those teachers who have a disabled child studying in their schools.

The Research Site

The research site is in a drought prone area in Osmanabad district. This area is so isolated and so backward that most people know virtually nothing about it. When I mentioned to some friends that I am working in Osmanabad, they wondered if I was migrating to Pakistan! Average rainfall in this region is less that 30 cm per year and there is an acute shortage of water. Irrigation is available only in selected areas and most villagers live in conditions of extreme poverty. The majority of the population consists of landless labourers who migrate to cities after harvest. In fact, most families do not have sustainable income from farm work and the earning male members are generally employed away from the village (in most cases they come to Mumbai). Women, young children and old men dominate the village population. The average family size is six and 17 per cent of children are below the age of ten. School dropout rates are very high. In fact, since families have not seen the fruits of education in terms of tangible benefits, such as better income and permanency of job opportunities, they are not able to appreciate the importance of education.

The unspoken promise of education—'do well in school and you will get a good, well paying job in the future'—has not reached this region.

Women in the village spend substantial portions of their day fetching water, cleaning and cooking. There is very little free time for other activities like taking children to school. Until recently, schools were available only in a few villages and the average distance from the school was over 6 km. Access to school was the major hindrance to achieving and sustaining school admission. This was the main reason for children with special needs being left out of education. With the introduction of DPEP there is now a school in every village.

At present, the concentration is on an area of about 15 sq km, 40 km from Sholapur. The two small clusters of 23 villages comprise a population of approximately 32,000. Two villages are large and have a population of 3,482 and 3,645 respectively, due to their proximity to cities. All others have a population of less than 800. There is only one special school, for the hearing impaired, in the neighbourhood with educational facilities for 7 years of schooling.

Some relevant observations about the clusters follow. Polio is the most crippling disease in these villages. In a selected area of six villages, out of 54 children with disability, 29 have polio. All these children are less than 5 years of age. The majority of these children (18) have minimal physical disability, only a limp in most cases, but they were outside the preschool education network. Sixteen of these are girls and all except one are outside the school.

Although primary health services and immunisation facilities are available locally, a little over a third of the 1,300 children under 5 years of age were not immunised at all or had received only partial immunisation. (Local authorities were alerted and we were promised that necessary steps would be taken to ensure 100 per cent immunisation.)

Preschool education service—anganwadis—have been set up in all the villages. The *balsevika* or preschool teacher knows all the children in the community and often has personal contacts with the family. Norms have been relaxed for this area and special units have been opened. In two villages where anganwadis could not be sustained, due to non-availability of teachers, now there are plans for starting *balwadi* services.

There appears to be no sex bias. In fact, the number of girls regularly attending anganwadis is slightly more than the boys. This is possibly because boys are expected to participate in the income generating activity while girls stay in the schools until they are married.

In one of the clusters some NGOs are working on developmental issues. Although they have no experience in working with children with special needs, they have shown interest and inclination to co-operate with SSI. There is a need for follow-up in order to ensure inter-agency co-operation.

Attitudes to Inclusive Education

It has been observed the children in their natural surroundings and studied reactions to inclusion from different groups. These observations are summarised below.

Families, especially mothers, make no attempt to enrol children with special educational needs in school. The common reason given for the exclusion was that the child has to be carried to school and there was no time for doing so. Some mothers pointed out that they realised the importance of being with their children during school hours and it was not possible to do so. With the setting up of schools at all villages, accessibility is increasing. This is leading to improved enrolments as reflected in an increase in the number of disabled attending school in some villages. In fact, 123 disabled children are now attending schools. There are 12 children who do not attend anganwadis as against 21 who do!

The head of the village, sarpanch, is the opinion leader. If he is trained and educated on the issues of inclusion, he takes a lead in changing community attitudes. The headmaster of the school is an influential person and also helps in creating awareness. In 14 villages, the headmaster himself is the sarpanch. There was no need, therefore, to further convince him about giving education opportunities to children with special needs.

Since the villagers depend on manual work as the main, and in many cases only, source of income, disability assumes a different dimension. Mild impairments including deafness, speech deficits and mild intellectual retardation are not considered disabilities. Therefore, 50 per cent of the disabled population is readily 'integrated' because they are involved in some form of income-generating activity.

Persons with severe physical disabilities are looked upon as liabilities and are discriminated against. There is a tendency to assume that those persons who cannot contribute to income generation are 'mental' or mad. They are not given opportunities for skill development or education. Their opinions and in fact they themselves are never considered.

Education officers are not aware of the change in policy and the shift towards inclusive education and assume that it is not going to be possible to educate disabled children within the normal school system. There is need for a focused training programme for them. Schoolteachers are not negative about the idea of inclusive education but they do not see their role in a wider perspective. Teachers whom we spoke to expressed willingness to have children with special needs in their classes, although they did not know that they may have to upgrade their skills.

The DPEP directorate and state education department are unable to appreciate that the needs of different disability groups are very distinct. The state has made no provision for aids and appliances, treatment and therapy or special teaching aids. There is at present no plan for upgrading teachers.

Concluding Summary

This project has evolved from a very modest objective. We have gained very rich experience and useful pointers. Some of them are:

- Good relationships with the local opinion leaders, parents of school children, families of disabled children, teachers, AWWs and government officials are crucial for this developmental work. If the villagers feel threatened in any way there is an outright rejection of any idea.
- The role of the SSI researchers is only that of a catalyst, and the true owners of the project are the teachers and education officers in the area. They have to be actively involved in the process.
- The topic of financial incentives for teachers of the integrated classes was raised, but the inputs have not been stated clearly although the disability act of 1996 makes a mention of higher compensation for special teachers.
- Although training and development of manpower is the soundest personnel investment, no plan for teacher training and AWWs has been made.
- The present involvement is only on a short term basis. The state DPEP should take a medium to long term flexible approach to integration.

SSI has shown its willingness and ability to work creatively at different hierarchical levels. DPEP now must show its trust by reaching out to the field staff without imposing delays in implementation policy.

Note

1. I would like to express my sincere gratitude to Ms Mithu Alur, Founder and Chairperson of the SSI, for constant encouragement and support. My research associate, Ms Swapna Sengupta, has made a number of visits to the research site, has educated me on the socioeconomic details of the area and has co-ordinated with the local education authorities. Mr Shravan Shirture has collected data from the field, which were very valuable for the report.

7

From Integration to Inclusive Education: Seva-in-Action

Ruma Banerjee

There is nothing like a dream to create the future.
—Victor Hugo

Introduction

The following is an attempt to describe the world of children with disabilities as it exists here in Seva-in-Action—a community-based rehabilitation and inclusive education programme—in the rural areas of Bangalore and Kolar district of Karnataka. It is an attempt to understand children's world in the context of related educational structures that determine their lives, their development and individual growth and to promote the right of children to go to school.

In the past, large resources were invested in special schools and institutions for children with disabilities but without reaching more than a fraction of those in need. Nowhere in the world has education in specialised settings been found for helping these children. Having abandoned the miracle solution for educating children with disabilities, more realistic and practical approaches to education have been looked for and have eventually emerged.

Inclusive Education

Though inclusive education has become a concept on the lips of many professionals working in the field, as previously was the concept of integration, in most situations children with disabilities are already in regular schools; they have not been segregated. Some have gone to school and others have not.

The term inclusive education is more than a term. It means to welcome all children without discrimination into the regular school. According to international conventions, such as the Salamanca Declaration from 1994, inclusive education is a human right.

From Integration to Inclusive Education

According to the 1991 Census, the total population of the district is four million. Children form 12 per cent of the total population. According to a systematic survey conducted by the Government of Karnataka in 1993, 6 per cent of the child population is in need of some special support in the age group 0–14 years.

The high prevalence of malnutrition due to poverty requires major attention in these areas. Disability is not a priority problem due to the existence of other pressing problems.

Basic Structure of Seva-in-Action (SIA)

SIA is a community-based rehabilitation programme which has made an attempt to prepare the community to meet the needs of people with disabilities using the existing infrastructure and resources of the community. SIA was started in 1985 in Bangalore rural district. It has initiated village-level CBR committees which are responsible for planning and managing the programme. Inclusive education is an integral part of the Seva-in-Action programme. The programme is being conducted in seven schools in eleven taluks of two districts. There are 490 disabled children including physically disabled.

Trained multipurpose resource teachers are the local persons in implementing the programme at the village level. The organised multipurpose self-help groups have seven objectives. These are:

- To identify children with special needs.
- To assist the facilitator in preparing them for mainstream education and employment.
- To meet their special educational needs in regular classrooms.
- To conduct resource teaching after class hours.
- To maintain a resource centre at the taluk level.
- To engage in curriculum adaptation for specific subjects.
- To assist the government school teachers during the time of evaluation.

Objectives of the Inclusive Education Programme

- To provide early intervention for disabled children and to train mothers, AWWs and CBR workers in early intervention programmes.
- To influence government programmes by assisting in training personnel to provide inclusive education through the DIET and assisting them to conduct similar training at district level.
- To assess children with special needs.

SIA has developed and tested a detailed survey format for identification of children in the age groups 0–6 and 6–14 years. The objective of the format is to identify and categorise children with disabilities.

Implementation of the Programme

SIA puts major emphasis on early intervention as successful integration also depends on this. The various approaches in early intervention are:

Home based	0–3 years
Self-help groups	3–6 years
Anganwadi centres	3–6 years

Self-help Group—Multipurpose Resource Centre

The self-help group—multipurpose disability centre uses any place that is available in villages, such as temples, community halls or regular schools. The self-help groups meet the needs of children in the age group of 3–6 years and prepare them for primary education. A self-help group also acts as preschool in villages where there are no preschools. It also trains children above 16 years in pre-vocational training.

Besides this, there is a resource centre to provide educational support to children integrated into regular schools. The resource centre is equipped with the teaching and aids required for these children.

After the child is prepared and reaches cognitive level of 6 years, they are integrated into regular schools. There is regular support by the resource teachers to these children. The teacher visits the school regularly. Children also receive resource teaching before or after school hours. Resource centres are established at taluk level in regular schools or in the place given by the community. These centres are equipped to meet the needs of these children through special facilities and teaching aids.

After planning the curriculum, the method used is behaviour modification techniques with all disabled children. These children are prepared for integration in regular schools; if they are not eligible for integration, which happens particularly with moderate and severe categories of mental retardation, they are entered for vocational training (see Figure 7.1).

The education system is the only infrastructure which is available in every village of India. No other support system for rehabilitation exists in rural areas.

As far as caring is concerned, the Indian family with its closely knit structure gives a caring environment to the majority of their children. Thus SIA has been able to utilise this strength and has made self-help groups a forum to bring families together in planning and managing the programmes. The family members are members of local CBR committees which are totally responsible for running the programmes at community level. The parents have been trained through workshops in managing their disabled child at home. They are also responsible for providing a monitoring support to the CBR teacher.

Figure 7.1: Monitoring mechanism

CHILD
Initial Assessment by Resource Teacher
Tool: Based on the curriculum

Weekly Monitoring Programme by Resource Teachers
Tool: Same as above

Monthly Monitoring by Field Co-ordinators

Monthly Monitoring by Local Committees and Field Co-ordinator
Tool: Monitoring records by SIA based on MLL

Tool: Annual plans/objectives monthly reports: Quarterly Evaluation Director

Partnership with the Community

CBR builds on the strengths and potential inherent in the community. In SIA, CBR committees are the backbone of the programme. There are 11 CBR committees in the rural areas of Bangalore district to plan, implement and evaluate CBR programmes. These committees have been formed by local people from different backgrounds—teachers, doctors, principals of schools, social workers, agriculturists, members of women's organisations and also parents of disabled people. These committees have come together as they have social concern for children with disabilities.

SIA seeks to tap the strengths inherent in the community for sustaining CBR programmes. The major responsibility of the community is to mobilise resources, and plan and implement programmes at the community level. The community is also being prepared to monitor the rehabilitation service so that there is less dependence on professionals at district level.

UNESCO Teacher Education Resource Pack

SIA has been using the UNESCO Resource Pack in the training programmes on inclusive education. Our training co-ordinator has been using
this Pack and has received a good response from in-service teachers during
the training period. But there is no follow up after training. She feels it is
easy to use the Resource Pack with teachers and make them rethink
their practice in their own classrooms. Enjoyable learning can be provided
and leads trainees to take responsibility for their own learning. She herself
is enjoying teaching with the Resource Pack.

Plan of Action for Inclusive Education Developed by DSERT in Karnataka

India is one of the signatories in the 1990 world summit. This has resulted
in the formulation of policies and plans of action which recognise the
rights of the children on the nations economic resources. These planning
measures are initiated by concerned departments in the government such
as health, primary education and welfare. The needs of children with
disabilities are seen as one of the focused special issues in planning.

The National Policy on Education 1986 lays special emphasis on the
removal of disparities and the need to equalise educational opportunity
by attending to the specific wants of those who have so far been denied
equal opportunities. Outlining the steps for ensuring equal educational
opportunities to disabled children, the National Policy on Education (NPE)
states that the objective should be to integrate the physically and mentally
handicapped with the general community as equals, prepare them for
normal growth and enable them to face life with courage and confidence.

The NPE's plan of action was used as the guideline in preparing
Karnataka's Plan of Action for children in 1992. Based on the national
policy, a programme of action was developed which focused on universalisation of elementary education and integrated education of disabled
children by 2000. In 1996, a draft Plan of Action was prepared by the
Integrated Education for Children with Disabilities Advisory Committee
(which was set up by the education minister in 1992). The Plan on inclusive
education was jointly prepared by the government and voluntary organisations in February 1996.

Objectives of Inclusive Education in Karnataka State

1. To enrol all disabled children in general schools by 2001 AD.
2. To prescribe minimum levels of learning with adaptations in the curriculum for disabled children in general schools.
3. To reduce the number of dropouts of disabled children in IED schools—general and special.
4. To provide access to secondary education for disabled children with resource support.
5. To provide access to vocational training for children with intellectual disabilities both in special schools and IED general schools.
6. To focus on developing manpower training requirements at pre-service and in-service teacher education in order to meet the special needs of disabled children in general schools.
7. To provide access to education and vocational training for disabled children and other deprived children, through NFE programmes.
8. To extend educational and vocational services for disabled adults through adult education.

To achieve the above objectives in rural Karnataka, a scheme has to be drawn to promote CBR for all disabled persons by 2001 AD.[1]

Problems and Major Issues

The community has played an extremely important role in sustaining the SIA programme. During the decade of SIA programme there has been a considerable change in attitude towards disability.

Some of the major problems faced by us are:

- Sub-standard government schools.
- Lack of positive attitude on the part of policy makers towards education of disabled children.
- Prescriptive curriculum in primary schools and compulsory levelling of all children.
- Special education still being planned on disability labels rather than on ability levels.
- Wide dispersion of disabled children in rural and tribal areas.

- Complex associations between poverty and disability where mothers are over burdened with fieldwork/housework and the demands of bringing up a disabled child.
- A classroom for all is still a dream which is yet to be achieved in Indian village schools.
- Single-teacher schools which are generally viewed as a crippling factor for integrated education seen as a plus point by SIA as it allows mixed ability level learning!
- The basic issue is the time constraint with the parents and the community. As majority of the parents are dependent on agriculture and self employment, each and every minute is invaluable towards sustaining their livelihood and meeting their basic needs, and they are not able to give time to the child.
- Availability of trained personnel at middle management.
- Monitoring of programmes by trained personnel is one of the major issues to sustain quality. This is a necessary evil to maintain the quality of services.

Lesson Learnt

- The best possible support should be available at the village level—90 per cent of special educational needs should be met at the community level.
- Integrated education should be seen as an entry point to improve the existing primary education.
- Inclusive schools with inclusive curriculum and teachers are the best way of achieving cost effective solutions.
- The government has set an advisory committee for IED. This committee has played a major role in bringing about policy changes and integrated disability aspects in general teacher training programmes.
- In CBR people have the misconception that there is no need to look at special educational needs. It is important that CBR programmes should see IED as an integral component since 80 per cent of the needs of children with disabilities are educational needs rather than medical.

Trained resource teachers should be given priority in appointments for implementing inclusive education.

Note

1. Source: Department of State Education and Training (1996) B.P. Wadia Road, Basavangudi, Bangalore.

8

Inclusive Education Experiences

Pearl Kavoori

In the course of my work, I met several people concerned with special education in one way or another, administrators and policy makers, professionals like physiotherapists, speech therapists and psychologists, social workers, social scientists, concerned citizens, theatre personalities with social sensitivity and, more importantly, mainstream educationists. All these people without exception showed not only positive interest in inclusive education, but also showed a sense of concern with the emerging challenges of special education. The involvement of the mainstream educationists, in fact, went beyond the conceptual aspects. They were trying to seek answers to the challenge of mainstreaming children with special needs, although most of them were not versed in it at the practical level. The concern, it is obvious, has become a live academic and professional issue.

I come from a mainstream education background with a continuing and rising interest in special education for almost 20 years. My chapter will be coloured by this background, though what I say will be confined to sharing my experiences and efforts.

The Delhi Experience

My first opportunity of dealing with children with special needs came while I was working with Bharatiya Vidya Bhawan, New Delhi. Bharatiya

Vidya Bhawan was a regular school with a progressive leadership given to innovative problem solving. The school was also well equipped with a well organised and fully-staffed counselling centre, strengthened by a sound staff development programme, geared to creating sensitivity.

Against the background that I have given of the regular school, the need was felt to start a special education centre for children with special needs. Soon after the decision to start this centre was taken, AIIMS gave us help for testing and assessment of children seeking admission to the centre.

The initial special education class of three students with mild to moderate impairments soon increased and fortunately a trained special educator was found to look after the children with special needs. Since the special education centre and the regular school were in the same building, the children of both streams began an unplanned and informal interaction. The beginning of the whole experience could be termed as *unintentional integration*. It was soon realised that this informal interaction was enhancing the self-esteem, confidence and social skills of students with disabilities and was promoting their acceptance by students of the regular school.

On this basis a planned programme of mainstreaming began. Integration was most successful in those classes where both the regular teacher and the special education staff were committed to the idea. Success of the programme was affected by several factors, e.g., number of students in the regular class, accommodation, correct time-tabling and availability of learning material, but the linchpins of success always were the attitude and sensitivity of the regular school teacher and the special education personnel when joint and mutually acceptable perceptions emerged between the two.

Both socialisation and learning took place during the school assembly, the school interval, the yoga, dance, painting and pottery classes in the library, the storytelling classes and the home science lab; but in the music class the experience remained unsatisfactory. On the play field, where one would expect easy integration to take place, disappointingly this did not happen. Competitiveness on the play field dulled the sensitivity of the regular students towards their peers with special needs. The P.E. teachers did not have the sensitivity to create alternative situations conducive to integration.

One of the significant aspects of this effort was that an insightful learning took place on the part of the teachers to make integration a success. Happily, a majority accepted the idea of integration and the need to implement it. The entire school family became palpably sensitive. This included the administrative staff also. In the entire experience, the most important elements were the attitude of the regular teacher and the enabling and helping role of the principal, the vice principal and the school counsellor.

The special education centre in Bharatiya Vidya Bhawan continues to work effectively and satisfactorily.

The Jaipur Experience

When Maharaja Sawai Man Singh Vidyalaya Learning Centre started in 1984, the idea of inclusion of children with special needs in the regular school was very much on the agenda. Due to various constraints the programme could not be started immediately. However, as part of the ongoing staff development programme, care was taken to include issues concerning the integration of children with special educational needs. Hence, by the time the actual programme of integration started, the staff were ready psychologically and academically.

A beginning of including children with learning disabilities in regular classes was made in 1990, when two students with low academic achievement and with social and emotional problems were admitted to the middle school. Three more students from regular classes were identified with similar problems. These students with special needs remained part of the regular classes but received individual attention in a few academic subjects. Careful assessment and planning guaranteed that each student followed an appropriate programme. Special school teachers gave up their free periods to work with these students. Support was provided and goals set for the year.

In order to work out this programme for the five students in the middle school, many time-table complexities had to be resolved. However, at the end of the year several difficulties came to light which pointed to changes that needed to be made. Regular teachers could not be expected to give up their free periods as other work suffered. More teaching aids and instructional material were needed. The help of a trained psychologist was required for correct assessment and lastly, but very importantly, the programme had to start from the very earliest classes.

Then the Learning Centre in the MSMS Vidyalaya started. With increased teaching aids and instructional material, a full time resource person, aided by part time resource persons with expertise in subjects depending on the special needs of students, was referred to the Learning Centre. Regular teachers filled in referral cards, and assessment services were provided by the British school psychologist. The entire effort was based on teamwork and co-operation, where the resource teachers, regular teacher, psychologist, the principal and the parents became partners through regular meetings and discussions.

The process of enlarging and developing the Special Learning Centre still continues. On an average, between 10 and 15 students are referred to the Special Learning Centre each year. They continue to study in the regular class and come to the centre depending on their special needs.

It is important to mention here that the teacher-in-charge of the Special Learning Centre is not a trained special educator but has a background of Montessori training, and care has been taken to prepare her for a more effective role. She has been exposed to effective and innovative methods of teaching by studying other such centres in the country.

It must also be mentioned that the leadership of the school has made a special effort to create continuous in-service training programmes for teachers, which has led to the creation of a sensitive and creative milieu in the school.

Comparison between the Two Experiences

The experiences of the two schools in Delhi and Jaipur—you can call them models—differed. The Bharatiya Vidya Bhawan experience centred round the creation of a special education centre alongside a regular school, whereas the MSMS Vidyalaya grew from within the school as an integral part of it and as part of a goal-oriented process of change and development. The two need different organisational co-operation inputs, to some of which I have already referred to.

There are common elements to both the experiences which I shall spell out briefly:

1. Democratic, forward-looking leadership with a sense of vision.
2. Ideological orientation towards a child-centred education.
3. Belief in staff development and training, not only for skill development but also for sensitivity of the staff to explore and innovate.
4. Confidence and willingness to raise resources.

5. Development of sensitivity in staff and children as a joint effort.
6. Teamwork and collective decision making.
7. Democratic functioning with decentralised responsibility.

The two experiences I have shared are micro level ones. I have not tried to cover the larger issues of integration which have been dealt with earlier. These could be called grass root experiences. They form the warp and woof of integration and are therefore truly useful to my fellow principals.

9

Culture-Specific Paradigms of Integration in Developing Countries

Usha Singh[1]

The history of rehabilitation and educational integration of the handicapped forms a remarkable chapter of human endeavour. In recent times there has been a great awakening among people regarding the need for meaningful treatment of children with various disabilities. Without this human touch and consideration the dreams they cherish will never be realised and, as educators, we can never feel we have given our best.

The Jaipur scenario has been similar to that in other cities where the early experiences of children have become so rigid that the child has little breathing room. Instead of the programme being child-oriented it is content-oriented. Mayura felt a growing concern for these children and this generated intense thinking on the future of education and children. Our activity-oriented system encouraged children to form the foundation of lifelong learning, and this interest is an asset that will stay with them the rest of their lives. To bring out the best in the child was our focus. We also realised that it was of prime importance for regular classroom teachers to be trained in diagnosing teaching strategies for children with learning disabilities because there were several children in many classes who could be identified as having learning problems, the reasons being various medical problems, dyslexia, aphasia or brain impairment, and the system causing tension and strain. Hence we began with remedial teaching practices. The enigma of the child who was unable to learn became our concern. Some children were unable to learn readily and exhibited hyperactive behaviour while others were withdrawn. Other children exhibited perceptual disturbances alongside their learning problems. We also realised that, by identifying these children as preschoolers before they encounter difficulty, it was possible to diagnose their disabilities and institute remedial education to prevent potential learning problems. Since children do not mature at the same rate, readiness for school often is a matter of timing. Some children had developmental lags that disappeared by the time they were ready for formal schooling.

Beena[2] was the first child, who came to us at the age of 5 in 1991 (diagnosed as a case of cerebral palsy). She was disabled, could not walk much or balance. Her hands were floppy too. She was dribbling and had a tendency to choke quickly. She joined a 3-year-old group. They accepted Beena beautifully as they were ever willing to make her comfortable. The teacher encouraged Beena to join in all the activities—reciting, singing, dancing, storytelling, drama, art, craft and games. Beena too had a strong urge and tremendous will power to do her best with great sincerity. Whatever she did, even if it was an attempt as a solo presentation, she received great applause and cheering from her teachers and friends. There was a transformation in Beena and within a few months, she was walking quite a distance from the main gate to her classroom, whereas initially she had to be carried. Beena never said 'I can't' or 'I won't', whether it meant dancing or racing. Her determination and inner strength led her on and she accepted the learning programme which included cognitive development, perceptual motor development, pre-academic skills and language development. She was also encouraged to take swimming classes. She is presently studying in Class III. She can comprehend well, read, write English and Hindi and do arithmetic, her concepts are very clear and she excels in computers. There are limitations due to time constraints in writing, but she is not willing to take a separate programme. Recently at a science exhibition, she took on the responsibility to present information about the human body, and faced the crowd with great confidence. She is ever willing and enthusiastic to take part in swimming, games, songs, dances and elocution. We are now planning her programme for the next few years using a computer. We are confident that Beena, like other children, will attain her goal and be honoured for her extraordinary will power and sincere efforts.

Gopi joined Mayura in July 1992 at the age of 3. He was declared a case of cerebral palsy and had difficulty in walking and standing. With physiotherapy, he improved but he has an awkwardness in gait. Although he was friendly, cheerful and self-confident, at times he was withdrawn and seemed disturbed. He exhibited symptoms of behavioural problems and learning problems. It was difficult to discern which handicap was primary, so we observed him carefully over a period of time, and his mother followed up his learning process at home too. Very soon Gopi progressed and did extremely well in sensory, motor and conceptual areas. He could comprehend and express well too. He had problems at the affective level—anxiety, emotional stability, attention, focus, task persistence and social behaviour. He is presently studying in Class II and doing well in academic work and activities such as games and swimming. He tends to get hyperactive and blow up easily, and at times is distracted from the tasks in hand. In the last few months he seems to have matured and has increased his ability to control himself. Gopi is very fond of his teachers and school. He is ever ready to do anything to be in school and he is always very direct and honest with his feelings. He needs to be handled with patience and love. All of this is like any other child and he will definitely do well in life.

Pamela (child with cerebral palsy) joined Mayura at the age of 6 in July 1995. She could walk but had a high stoppage gait, poor motor co-ordination and excessive drooling. She was shy, reserved and dependent. She was with the 3-year-old group. She had problems in language and cognitive skills, disturbances in perception, limited speech, and social and emotional behaviour. This impeded the normal learning process. She was unable to organise materials and could not comprehend or follow instructions. She was easily distracted and had limitations in fine motor skills too.

Since she joined school, she has progressed, mainly because she enjoys coming to school and is cheerful, enthusiastic and confident. She enjoys the school schedule although it is structured at times. She eats independently. She takes interest in colouring, scribbling, games, singing and dancing. She can follow instructions and makes an effort to say sentences too. Of late she enjoys tracing and loves matching shapes and letters. She is keen on doing these activities at home too. She helps her mother with small errands. All parents have been extremely co-operative during the process of adjustment.

Two other children, Mohan and Nitin, come from local pre-primary schools. Both the parents felt that the pressure on them, especially to produce written work, has affected them and hence they were not motivated to learn. Both of them were normal in every way. They could read, write and do arithmetic like any average student. But within a few months we observed that they exhibited hyperactive behaviour, were easily distracted and continuously in motion (with Mohan it took 2 years to come to a conclusion). They were emotionally disturbed and disruptive. Since Disha had come into existence, before we came to conclusions, we referred them to Ms Deepak Kalra. They were assessed and both had slight mental retardation. Mohan is presently with Disha and Nitin is still with us.

Ali was another child with a physical disability. One hand (left) was short. He came to us in the nursery group. He was withdrawn and shy but today he has developed so much self confidence that he is doing extremely well both in academic work and co-curricular activities. Praise and the opportunities given to him in presentations helped him feel positive about himself.

Ajit (affected by muscular degenerative disease) joined Mayura at the Class III level in 1994. He could walk with help. Children helped him to go to the assembly area and art and music classes. He did not have any problem with academic work. He left after a year due to his father's transfer. He rejoined Mayura in 1996–97 session at Class VI level. He has to be carried with the help of an attendant. The advantage of being here is that he did not have to use the staircase to attend any class. He was given the opportunity to participate in the elocution competition. The children see to his needs and help by providing books from the library during the games period. He is not able to keep up with the writing work at times, but he has been doing very well in academic work. He has accepted his condition as a way of life and is never seen or heard to be unhappy with anyone or anything.

There are many more that one could talk about and these very children could have been ignored, labelled as failures, misdiagnosed by specialists, misunderstood by parents, teachers and often discarded by society.

The success of a mainstreaming programme is strongly influenced by teacher attitudes. So we stress:

1. In-service education which is an essential preparation for main-streaming programmes.
2. Pupil placements that call for sensitive administration, educational assessment and diagnostic teaching.
3. A programme that is flexible and can be modified.

The entire experience has been a challenge and extremely rewarding because we felt that we were extending to these children the full dignity of a human being.

We can have very lofty ideals, but to implement them we need sincere, dedicated hands not just qualified persons. The government and voluntary sectors should come forward to help the institutions wedded to this cause by sponsoring candidates for training at other places and share the latest developments in education and technology. This could be done through conferences and by encouraging the exchange of personnel.

Notes

1. I am extremely grateful and indebted to Disha, Ms Kavoori and Ms Kalra for their support and guidance. The very existence of Disha is a beacon light to many. I hope we can work together with the provision for research, training of education personnel and the development of model centres in the fields of learning disabilities and handicapped children.
2. The names of the children have been changed deliberately.

10

Towards Equalisation of Opportunity for Children with Special Needs

P.T. Augustine

The central thrust of this book is integration as opposed to segregation of disabled children from children with a normal range of ability. My knowledge of and experience with institutions that provide education to the mentally handicapped in either a segregated or integrated set-up are extremely limited. However, I would like to state that I am open to new ideas and approaches that seek to explore the equalisation of opportunities for various sections of society, especially children with special needs.

Permit me to cite an instance of experimentation with integration of various strata of society that the Jesuit Schools (St. Xavier's Schools in North India and, more specifically, St. Xavier's School, Jaipur) have undertaken in the recent past. Broadly termed as our 'option for the poor', this new educational policy of our schools involved basically three elements:

1. For initial admission to the school, reservation of at least 25 per cent of places to the poor section of society, providing them with scholarships and financial assistance, and helping them to cope academically with the studies by arranging a 2-year Balwadi programme before admission and remedial classes during the 12 years of studies in our school.

2. Adoption of a bilingual pattern of education with Hindi as the medium of instruction at the primary level with sufficient emphasis on English, bilingual pattern at the middle school level and, thereafter, English as the medium for the rest of the classes.
3. Phasing out of boarding facilities and enabling more citizens of the city itself to benefit from our educational facilities.

However, our option for the poor is not an exclusive option but a special concern for the poor and the underprivileged. What we are aiming at is an education that will integrate the various sections of society by providing more of the weaker sections of society an opportunity for good education, which is the biggest and most effective single factor for equalisation. This small step will help in its own measure to move away from a dual society that divides our people between the rich and the poor, the powerful and the powerless, the established and the marginalised.

The first 7 to 8 years of the new educational policy was a struggle marked by opposition from almost all sections, and for us frustration and disappointments. But our persistence and perseverance paid dividends. Today we certainly can take some credit for initiating an educational pattern that some way contributes to the integration of the various sections of society. I must also add that people who were opposed to our new policy for several years have also come to acknowledge today its positive impact on society.

Having successfully gone through the agonising search for one type of integration, we have the confidence today to take the first step towards another type of integration, namely, integration of the educable mentally retarded into the mainstream of society through education. This does not mean that I do not recognise the almost insurmountable problems and obstacles to this type of inclusive education. Society prejudices against interaction between retarded children and non-retarded children are certainly strong. There may also be some superstitious beliefs regarding the cause of mental retardation. Lack of special infrastructural facilities, shortage of trained and experienced personnel, fear of the loss of prestige for institutions, etc., are some of the other problems that come in the way of the inclusive pattern.

However, I believe that breaking down the barriers between handicapped and normal children is beneficial to both categories of children and will foster the development of a more integrated society.

Like all changes in society, especially a traditional society like ours, the change from exclusion to inclusion will be painful and will involve struggle, frustration and disappointments. But those with a vision of a more integrated society and those who have accepted education as a mission must face these challenges and find creative new ways to bring about social integration. In the context of the educable mentally retarded, what is required perhaps is not acceptance of a few EMR children into a normal school as a matter of *charity*, which we probably have been doing from time to time, but opening our doors and our hearts to the section of society as a personal and institutional *policy*, as a personal and institutional *commitment*. This certainly requires a change of heart and a change of attitude.

I believe that schools like St. Xavier's and other leading schools of Jaipur could come forward to take the first step and be trailblazers in the field of education for children with special needs.

11

Inclusive Education: The Jaipur Experience

Deepak Kalra

It has been very informative and interesting to hear about the experiences of various schools in Jaipur, and encouraging and heartening to hear about the interventions being made for inclusive education. The students and the teachers involved in this need to be congratulated as they have proved to us that if we try, we can have successful inclusive education in the schools of Jaipur. These efforts should move and motivate many and give them the confidence to make a beginning towards inclusive education.

This chapter discusses the other side of the coin. It is the story of children who have not been so fortunate as to be absorbed into the mainstream; they have either not gained admission to school or have dropped out of school for various reasons. My chapter is based on the experience of 50 children with special needs who are presently studying in Disha Centre for special education since 1995. The age, sex and disability distribution of the sample is as follows (also see Table 11.1):

Male: 29
Female: 21
Age group: 6–20 years

Table 11.1: Disability distribution of children with special needs in Disha Centre

Type of Disability	Number
Cerebral Palsy	20
Downs Syndrome	8
Minimal Brain Dysfunction	13
Hydrocephaly	2
Microcephaly	1
Post Meningitis	1
Others	3
Total	**48**

As Disha started only two years back, since 1995, and is the first of its kind in Rajasthan it is interesting to note the educational background of these students (Table 11.2).

Table 11.2: Educational background of children with special needs in Disha Centre

Category	Number
Never attended school before	19
Attended special school	9
Attended special school and dropped out	2
Dropped out of normal schools	17
Private tuition	3
Total	**50**

Nineteen students who did not attend any school before Disha were between the ages of 6 and 15 years. The reason given by parents for not attending any school was either

1. the parents did not feel that any school would give them admission and did not try, or
2. in most cases admission was refused for reasons like the child did not speak, was not intelligent enough to cope, was hyperactive, or was not toilet trained.

In the case of six students, parents were told that parents of other children would object to these children or the reputation of the school would be affected.

Eleven attended special schools, but were not at all satisfied as the schools did not have any trained staff, the student-teacher ratio was not met, individual planning was not done, in fact hardly any activities were conducted and parents were totally dissatisfied. Two dropped out for similar reasons and the other nine carried on waiting for an alternative. The majority of the students on our waiting list are also from special schools.

Twenty went to regular schools, of whom three dropped out and took private tuition at home at a very early age. Seventeen remained in normal schools for periods ranging from 2 years to 11 years.

An analysis of the dropouts from normal schools indicated the following reasons:

1. Failed for several years and asked by school authorities to leave.
2. Not promoted to senior classes beyond nursery.
3. Isolated and neglected in classes, just left alone and not included in any programme including educational programme.
4. Showed hyperactive behaviour and behaviour problems and asked to leave.

Some reasons given by students were:

5. Friends teased when they failed.
6. Teacher never waited for the student to finish and rubbed the blackboard.
7. Felt very isolated, had no friends.
8. It was very embarrassing to be in junior class.

When children failed none of them was tested to find out the reason for failing, e.g., any specific learning disability, learning gaps or emotional problems. Instead the parents were called and warned that the child would be removed from school if s/he failed. The parents started private coaching—2 to 4 hours a day after school in most cases—which made matters worse.

It may not be presumptuous to deduce from the above that if care and support were given at the time the child failed, s/he would not have dropped out. Preventing a child from dropping out from a normal school can be the first step all schools can take towards inclusive education. Some suggestions to prevent students from dropping out are listed below:

1. The reason for failure should be established and support provided accordingly, e.g., remediation for special learning disability, individual session with subject teacher in case there is a learning gap and so on.

2. Special needs of children could be met through consultation services of consultants/psychologists/resource teachers, etc.
3. Workshops could be held to sensitise teachers and students.
4. A resource cell could be set up in each school to reach out to the special needs of children.

As is said, prevention is better than cure. Inclusive education can begin by preventing students from dropping out of schools.

12

Integrated Education: Reflections on the Calcutta Experience

Reena Sen

This chapter focuses on two aspects of integrated education for students with multiple disabilities. The first deals with the current status of integrated education in Calcutta and the districts of West Bengal. The second focuses on issues to do with school reform and classroom management which I see as being essential and critical factors for integrated education to be truly inclusive. I would like to clarify that in this chapter I have discussed integration specifically from the point of view of students with special needs being educated full time in mainstream schools and have, therefore, not included programmes of partial integration of disabled peer groups. Another important point is that I do believe that not every student with cerebral palsy can be placed in a mainstream school and there will always have to be provision in special schools for those whose difficulties are severe or profound.

The Government of West Bengal has started working on the DPEP and there are plans for integrated education in the districts. Teacher training initiatives are also being discussed. A more positive climate for attitudinal and social change prevails but it is vital to move on from planning to the adoption of clear-cut policies and set clear and measurable objectives for translating policy into practice. It is equally necessary to define 'integrated education', as it is interpreted differently by different people.

As we all know, the number of disabled students in a school tells us nothing about the quality of their educational experiences and simply sitting in a class does not ensure one is learning.

At present, particularly in the context of students with cerebral palsy, education in mainstream schools in Calcutta and neighbouring districts can best be described as a bonus rather than a right. There is no explicit policy which makes it mandatory for schools to give admission. Therefore, the student gets a place when there is a kind and sympathetic headteacher and if the student can walk with or without aid, has functional speech, no severe sensory deficits, is independent in eating, drinking and using the toilet and, most importantly, can cope with the syllabus—in short, as long as the school does not have to make any significant adaptations to the physical environment or the curriculum. Writing difficulties frequently pose problems, particularly in the middle and senior classes, but permission to use a typewriter or a writer or extra time during examinations is not obtained without considerable debate and much persuasion. Examination boards do give these exemptions but the process of obtaining permission is lengthy and laborious and each case is considered on an individual basis. Much relief has been provided by the National Open School which enables students to appear for less subjects and over a number of years, but most mainstream schools do not offer this option, so the students have to drop out of the mainstream in order to avail of the open school system. I do not mean to undermine the many examples of good practice in schools which have admitted students with cerebral palsy where headteachers and teachers have been co-operative and supportive, but there is urgent need of definite policies and for building up the necessary infrastructural support systems to meet the special and individual needs of students. This is essential if we are to educate these children. As Seamus Hegarty has said, 'Students with special needs do not need integration. They need education' (Hegarty et al., 1981).

This brings me to the second aspect of the chapter, which focuses on school reform. During 1993 and 1994, I had the opportunity of conducting both systematic and interpretative observations of 29 high, average and low achieving readers in 11 classrooms of Class 1 in six mainstream schools over one academic year. What emerged very clearly from the analysis of qualitative data was that the experience of individual children in the same classroom differed considerably and teacher focus on individual students was relatively infrequent. Second, the needs of low achievers were generally not met within the classroom.

Non-parametric statistical analysis of data from systematic observation indicated that 'lost and confused' behaviours were significantly higher in low achieving readers as a group in comparison with average and high groups. Informal conversations with teachers suggested that they felt that large class sizes and the rigid syllabus made it impossible to provide within-class support. It is easy to blame schools and teachers but one needs to keep in mind certain factors. First, our general teacher training courses equip teachers mainly for whole-class teaching. Second, schools are generally housed in buildings in which adaptations for physical access are hugely expensive. Last, and perhaps most significantly, there are huge numbers in the classroom with one teacher, the loaded inflexible syllabus and our strictly examination-oriented, high pressured, fiercely competitive education system.

Under these circumstances, my question is—If the special needs of non-disabled children are not met in the classroom, how do we ensure that the needs of those who have multiple disabilities will be met? If we are truly committed to inclusive education, we must work on the following priorities:

1. Developing methodologies for differentiation in curriculum delivery in classrooms in recognition of the heterogeneity of students.
2. Review and modification of the content of initial and in-service teacher training courses so that strategies for meeting individual needs within a group and using co-operative learning approaches become integral to classroom teaching.
3. Considering parents as valuable resources for the provision of within-class support to children with special needs and designing short training programmes for them as necessary.
4. Building up clear strategies for closer liaison between researchers and professionals in special education and educators in the mainstream and clearly stating the objectives and the expected outcomes of this collaboration and dialogue in terms of educational practice.
5. Grants-in-aid for schools to undertake structural adaptations and employ qualified resource teachers.
6. Including integrated education as a responsibility of the Ministry of Human Resource Development, Department of Education.

There are two further issues. First, while we work for more inclusive education we must continue to develop our special schools as richly resourced information, demonstration and training centres and to meet the needs of students with profound and multiple impairments and learning difficulties. Second, and this is in response to the comment that the best NGOs are those who do not seek government funding but rather those who work for a 'cause'. I believe that 'cause', commitment and funds are closely interrelated. If you are a parents' group working in Manipur or community workers in Birbhum or Murshidabad, you simply cannot go forward without funds. Therefore, if educational change is to become a reality, along with knowledge and commitment, there must be adequate funding from all possible sources—the government, international agencies and the community at large.

Reference

Hegarty, S., K. Pocklington and D. Lucas (1981) *Educating Pupils with Special Needs in the Ordinary Schools*. Windsor: NFER-NELSON.

13

Whole-School Approach and Curriculum Modification

Sudesh Mukhopadhyay

Introduction

School effectiveness and school development have always been a concern of practitioners and planners. Up until the 1990s, research and interventions have been initiated by experts and planners from outside the school. Slowly, however, it has been realised that innovations and changes imposed from outside have very limited impact on what happens in schools. This has resulted in a tendency for school improvement efforts to come from within the school and has led to terms such as the developing school and the creative school. This is based on the belief that schools will improve slowly, if at all, when reforms are thrust upon them. Rather, the approach having most promise, in my judgement, is one that will seek to cultivate the capacity of schools to deal with their own problems, to become largely self-renewing.

Research on these topics has helped to generate a few guiding principles for all those schools who want to initiate change from within. These can be listed as follows:

1. School development is a lengthy process and not an overnight, once-and-for-all event.
2. It is not a document written at one time but the recording of staff deliberations and planning decisions over a period of time.
3. It is a public document available for reference, sharing and negotiation.
4. It evolves over time to guide the implementation plan.
5. It is a mixture of vision and strategic planning that entails prioritising needs and preparing action plans on an ongoing basis.
6. It is a mixture of long term and short term perspectives.
7. Staff development is an integral part of the process.
8. There are three interlinked stages in the whole process—What are we searching for? Where do we want to be? How do we get there?
9. These stages are followed by an evaluation stage—How are we doing?

Whole-School Approach

This process is called a whole-school approach because it entails the full range of factors involved in bringing about change in schools. Whole-school development planning was initially regarded by many teachers as an additional burden. However, the continuous process of participation and the need to internalise external change have changed this attitude. Most of the activities in a school are related ultimately to what happens in the classroom where the teacher is the most powerful figure.

The whole-school approach is one of the most powerful approaches of the day to generate and internalise innovation for the improvement of the school. However, I would like to draw attention to the needs of the children who are part of this approach not only as beneficiaries but also as participants who can contribute to improving practice. The majority of schools would claim that their plans are intended to improve educational provision for children. However, a review should look for evidence rather than rhetoric. Therefore, reviews should look closely at the received curriculum and at children's work as process and product. This will be particularly true as schools move into their second cycle of drafting school development plans because these should be based upon a review of the first development plan and its implementation and success in terms of the children's activities.

If I have to interpret the whole-school approach in the context of policy and planning for the integrated education of disabled children then I would like to strengthen my case by quoting a direct experience of working for the mainstreaming of children with visual impairments in the regular classroom.

Whole-School Approach and Curriculum Modification

The National Policy on Education 1986 and the programme of action have visualised serving as many of these children as possible (mainly mildly handicapped) in regular schools. Special schools are to continue to provide facilities for severely disabled children. These provisions in policy documents call for schools to acknowledge the constitutional rights of disabled children as well as making their life as normal as possible.

A sample provision of facilities does not necessarily ensure effective implementation. Many educators at all levels are perplexed as to how to meet their responsibilities in the light of

- overcrowded classrooms,
- teachers not trained to handle and educate disabled children,
- danger of harming children's education in the absence of appropriate preparation,
- existing rules and regulations regarding school admission and evaluation which may not be suited to disabled children,
- absence of infrastructure at university and college level to prepare teachers for these new responsibilities, and
- social and political pressures to enrol these children in regular classrooms.

These are but a few of the problems being expressed by planners, educators, administrators and teachers.

Analysis of the above mentioned concerns would show that some are negotiable hurdles and some have to be endured. It was with this consideration in mind that the starting point was taken up as schools' commitment to integrate children with visual impairments. While other support was accepted as available, teachers were the main focus as the principal factor influencing the curriculum.

Understanding Special Needs of Children

It is necessary for every teacher to understand the learning styles of his/her students. Each student may have an individual approach to a learning situation. Some may be responding quickly and not too concerned to produce correct answers. Others may be reflective and analytic in nature, may take a lot of time to work on a task but like to produce correct answers only. Still others may be more mechanical and hesitant. But all these styles can be diagnosed in sighted as well as visually impaired children. Similarly, both types of children also get affected by sounds, group size, attention span and many such factors. Hence, there may be many commonalities that one can see between the learning styles of normal and disabled children. But there are certain special features associated with the learning of blind children because they are deprived of the visual sense. A teacher dealing with visually impaired children, especially in regular classrooms, must be aware of these features as the first step towards adjusting/adapting instruction to their needs.

Teachers also need inputs on seeing the relationship between the learning process and children's special needs, like impact of impairment, restricted experiences, level of maturation and role of incidental learning. This can be achieved through orientation programmes and exposure to learners (video films, literature). But the guiding principle is that neither the special needs of these children nor of the other children should lose out on learning because of integration. If multisensory approaches really were followed in schools, one would not be discussing these issues at all.

However, it indicates a possible strategy that teachers can follow to give optimum opportunities to all in the classroom. These are:

- duplicate as far as possible,
- modify without changing concept,
- substitute giving approximately same experience, and
- omit under unavoidable circumstances.

These were worked out especially for visually impaired children in the following manner:

- Compensatory experiences through additional verbal instruction,
- compensatory experience through the provision of appropriate learning materials in tactile form,

- compensatory experience through the provision of three-dimensional aids,
- compensatory experience through the creation of life situations,
- compensatory experience through auditory information supplemented by verbal explanation, and
- compensatory experience through all remaining faculties which do not demand vision as the primary source of input information.

In a classroom setting, a teacher cannot use one particular approach for providing the necessary learning experience, but may have to use all the above approaches in an integrated manner according to the different situations.

The analysis for developing an instructional strategy may be in terms of (a) instructional objectives for covering the components and sub-components of the learning task, (b) the components and sub-components of the learning task, (c) the learning experiences which can be provided by a regular classroom in a regular lesson alongside sighted children, (d) the learning experiences which will have to be provided in regular classrooms alongside instruction for sighted children with adjustment for sensory or cognitive deficits arising out of visual impairment, and (e) the learning experiences which will have to be provided to the visually impaired child outside a regular classroom, maybe in the resource room or actual life situations. The latter three types of learning experiences combined should help this child to learn optimally according to his or her capacities taking into account the deficits arising out of the disability.

This line of modifying curriculum was tried out by adapting/modifying the syllabi and curriculum in environmental studies for Classes 1–5. It is still being used in many schools in the south. Later on, this approach was used by NIVH to adapt the teaching of mathematics.

Implications for School

Though this approach refers to activities within the class, it has implications for the whole school. The school head can implement it only when the whole school accepts it. Having a child with a disability and giving him/her full educational opportunities entails decisions on location of classes, seating arrangements, planning of individual and group tasks, examinations and so on, not just in a single subject but in all subjects and classes. It cannot be the concern of one single person. Other students and parents are also involved. Thus, whole-school approaches and modifications to curriculum are complementary activities. In terms of processes, it involves all the steps mentioned in the introductory part of this presentation.

14

An Integrated School Experience

Amena Latif

I am a product of integrated education, having completed my schooling from Cathedral School, Mumbai. When I was three months old, my parents discovered that I had mild cerebral palsy. At home I was treated as a perfectly normal person and was encouraged to do everything for myself. This way I accepted the little disadvantages of not being able to run or do things swiftly without really feeling sorry for myself. Pre-primary education did not pose a problem. My twin sister and I went to the same nursery. However, it was felt that I might not be able to cope in the large school that my sister was admitted to and I was sent to a smaller school for my primary education. Secondary schooling was in the same school as my sister, though I was one class lower.

Right through my schooling I did not feel handicapped in any way, except for the fact that I could not participate in games. I discovered that my speed of writing was much slower than that of my classmates. Because of this I was given half an hour extra for each paper in my board exams. In school I was a girl guide and joined my classmates at various camps. Friends and classmates helped out with problems and my teachers were always encouraging and sensitive to my needs. I got to know much later that it was my mother who used to go to all the schools and talk to the principals, teachers and students before I joined any school.

After school I enrolled for the Nursery Teachers' Training Course at Sophia College as I always wanted to work with children. It was during this time that the confidence I acquired in school was further strength-ened. I started commuting by bus alone. The drawback I faced travelling alone was in crossing roads where I felt the necessity to seek someone's help as I tend to get startled by sudden noises and lose my balance and fall. Though people do sometimes mock my gait, they do rush to help when I fall. I have never really had a problem finding someone to help me to cross roads. As a child I have always feared crowds and walking among them. To overcome this my father used to take me for walks every evening in crowded areas to get the fear out of my system. I am thankful to my parents for keeping their fears from me and sharing their courage.

Perhaps the most significant step forward in my adult life. The path I chose. After my teacher training I met Ms Alur and got the opportunity to work with the Spastics Society of India. I was thrilled to bits. It was my ultimate dream come true. I have been with them for 20 years and have enjoyed every moment of it.

My fear of speaking has lessened since I joined the Spastics Society of India due to the encouragement and support Ms Alur gave me. She encouraged me to read poems and then longer pieces and then—horrors—give the vote of thanks for the convocations of the teacher training course. I am very grateful to her for the constant encouragement in my work and for giving me the opportunity of going abroad and doing an advanced diploma in Special Education.

I have spoken of my own childhood and experience as it has made me increasingly aware of the problems faced by disabled people and equally aware of how these can be handled in terms of support systems.

Fortunately, my problems not being so severe, I have not faced the problems faced by some of my students whom we would like to integrate. Barriers of access, transport, awareness and attitudes (see Chapter 22 in this volume). To overcome these barriers, at the Spastics Society of India, we have set up an advocacy and awareness cell. Its aims are:

- To enable or help the disabled and their families to stand up for their rights.
- To help parents and form a pressure group that could later bring about social policy changes.
- To help spread awareness about disability with specific reference to cerebral palsy.

We hope to do this through

- A media campaign whereby we reach out to the public with articles, stories, information and achievements related to disability issues.
- Street plays.
- A conference on inclusive education where educationists, principals and policy makers will debate issues related to integrated education.
- Independent living camps for the disabled.
- Training courses for the disabled on public speaking.
- A writers' club for disabled persons.
- Parent training programmes.

I'd just like to say that I feel convinced that if one makes up one's mind and is fortunate to have the encouragement and right opportunities, one gets the confidence to do almost anything.

PART II

International Perspectives on
Policy and Practice

15

International Policy and Practice in the Education of Disabled Children

Mark Vaughan

A Change in the International Climate of Opinion

On the international platform there have been a number of encouraging pronouncements in recent years, regarding the education of disabled children. The messages supporting inclusive education have never been stronger.

As a concept, special schools are at least 130 years old in the UK and elsewhere. For that time disabled children have been identified by an attribute that is beyond their control, and separated from their peer group for their education. We no longer have to do this! We have learned so much and travelled so far since the first philanthropic pioneers of Victorian times established these schools. Fundamentally, it is now a matter of human rights and social justice.

It appears to me that there is no long-term future for special schools, whether we look at the UK, Asia, North America, Europe or elsewhere. Later on in the chapter I will explain why I say that. For information, when I refer to disabled children, I mean all disabilities or learning difficulties.

UN Convention on the Rights of the Child 1989

The 1989 UN Convention on the Rights of the Child has been ratified by 177 countries world-wide. There are several general Articles in the Convention which lead up to Article 23, which is specifically about disabled children.

The Convention includes statement such as: all rights shall apply to *all* children, without discrimination on any ground *including disability*. In all actions the child's best interests shall be a primary *consideration* and they should develop to 'the maximum extent possible'. The Convention also states the right of the child to express an opinion and to have that opinion taken into account.

But it is Article 23 that covers disabled children saying the child's education shall lead to the *fullest possible social integration* and individual development, including his or her cultural and spiritual development. He or she shall have the right to enjoy a *full and decent* life, in conditions which ensure *dignity*, promote *self-reliance*, and facilitate the child's 'active participation in the community'. Article 23 also states the right of the disabled child to special care, education, health care, training, rehabilitation, employment preparation and recreation opportunities.

Furthermore, Articles 28 and 29, covering all children's education generally, say it shall be on the basis of equal opportunity; and that it should develop them to their 'fullest potential'. Education, says Article 29, should prepare a child for an 'active and responsible' life as an adult.

There are many values expressed by the UN Convention relevant to the struggle for inclusive education. I was grateful to hear a clear interpretation of the Convention given by a member of UN at CSIE's international human rights conference in London in 1995. Mr Thomus Hammarberg, Vice-Chair of the UN Committee of the Rights of the Child told the CSIE conference that the Convention was not just a list of dos and don'ts or a set of minimum requirements. It gave a firm attitude and philosophy towards children. He said: 'If you combine Articles 23—the disabled child's right to an active participation in the community—with Article 29, it follows logically that we are aiming for inclusive schools. Schools where there is a place for everyone's education and where everyone is welcome.' Mr Hammarberg said his Committee's interpretation of the Convention was very clearly one that favoured the goal of inclusive education for all.

UN Standard Rules 1993

I next turn to the UN Standard Rules on the Equalisation of Opportunities for Persons with Disabilities (1993). These Rules set an international standard for policy making and action covering disabled people. They give powerful support for the development of inclusive education for disabled pupils world-wide. In order to implement inclusive education, countries should have a 'clearly stated policy' that is understood at a school level and in the wider community.

States should recognise *principles of equal educational opportunities* for children, young people and adults with disabilities, in integrated settings. Rule 6, covering education, says that states should ensure that the education of disabled people is an integral part of the education system and it calls for

1. buildings to be accessible,
2. interpreter and other support services,
3. parents and organisations of disabled people to be involved in the education process,
4. a flexible curriculum plus additions and adaptations for disabled pupils, and
5. ongoing teacher training.

Where ordinary schools cannot yet make adequate provision to include disabled children, Rule 6 calls for 'special school education aimed at preparing the students for inclusion in the mainstream'.

UNESCO Salamanca Statement (1994)

In 1994, UNESCO, the UN's Education Agency, published the Salamanca Statement, a declaration on the education of disabled children, which called for inclusion to be the norm. Representatives of 92 governments and 25 international organisations agreed on it.

UNESCO's statement is unequivocal in asking the international community to endorse the approach of inclusive schooling: 'We call upon all Governments, and urge them to adopt as a matter of law or policy the principle of inclusive education, enrolling all children in regular schools, unless there are compelling reasons for doing otherwise.'

Disabled children 'must have access to regular schools' and it adds, for me, the most powerful paragraph in the whole document:

> Regular schools with this inclusive orientation are the most effective means of combating discriminatory attitudes, creating welcoming communities, building an inclusive society, and achieving education for all.
> Moreover, they provide an effective education to the majority of children and improve the efficiency and ultimately the cost-effectiveness of the entire education system.

The Salamanca Statement asks all governments to undertake a variety of actions, and I feel these could helpfully form the basis of the agenda for work to be done in very many countries, India included. It wants governments

- to give the highest policy and budgetary priority to improve education so all children can be included, regardless of individual difference or difficulties;
- to develop demonstration projects and encourage exchanges with countries which have inclusive schools;
- to ensure organisations of disabled people, along with parents and community bodies, are involved in planning and decision making; and
- to make early identification and intervention strategies a priority as well as vocational aspects of inclusive education and to ensure that both initial and in-service teacher training address the provision of inclusive education.

The Salamanca Statement calls for action from:

- UNESCO itself,
- UNICEF,
- the UN Development Programme, and
- the World Bank.

As the UN agency for education, UNESCO was specifically asked in the report to use its funds up to 2001 to create an expanded programme for inclusive schools and community support projects, thus enabling the launch of many pilot projects.

Salamanca says: 'In those countries with few or no special schools those countries should establish inclusive ordinary schools—not special schools, to serve disabled children.' And to finish this part on the Salamanca Statement, there is a quote in the report from a Swedish Member of Parliament, Mr Bengt Lindqvist:

> The challenge now is to formulate requirements of a school for all. All children and young people of the world have the right to education. It is not our education systems that have a right to certain types of children. It is the school system of a country that must be adjusted to meet the needs of all children.

India's Five Year Plan, 1991–96

India's Five Year Plan from 1991 to 1996 increased the budget for children with impairments by more than five times, and that India supports a major national development programme on the inclusion of disabled children in ordinary schools. I applaud this work and look forward to learning more about these developments.

The 1994 World Bank Report on Special Needs in the Asia Region, which looked at 15 countries including India, says that the development of inclusive primary education is the best option for achieving education for all in the Asia region by the year 2000. Universal Primary Education (UPE), it says, cannot be achieved without the inclusion of children with special needs. Disabled children can be 'successfully and much less expensively' accommodated in inclusive rather than segregated settings.

It's an important point about money! And as we know, economic arguments sway governments more than anything else! According to the report, if countries in the Asia region went down the segregation road for all disabled children, then costs would be enormous and prohibitive. Expanding a dual system of ordinary and special schools, like we did 100 years ago in the UK, is simply not appropriate.

If integrated, in-class provision with a support teachers system is envisaged for the vast majority of these children, then the additional costs can be 'marginal, if not negligible'. The report says India has major experience of absorbing children with special needs into ordinary classrooms, and providing appropriate training for teachers.

If we look at money for a moment the report says that in India the unit cost for children with special educational needs in mainstream schools is quoted as US\$ 6. Yet the unit cost for children with special needs in segregated settings is given as US\$ 33, five times the figure in mainstream. A child without special needs in the mainstream is given as US\$ 5.

The report says there are personal, social and economic dividends to be gained from inclusive education wherever possible. It concludes that a shift in philosophy is needed from a focus on deficits to an understanding that all children are capable of learning.

Reforms will be needed to teacher training if primary schools are to become truly inclusive; and the concluding messages of the World Bank Report are:

- Disabled children cannot be left out of the development of primary educational systems.
- It is vastly more expensive to segregate than to integrate.
- Major changes are needed in schools to support a more diverse range of learners.

An education minister of the Sudan visited CSIE 10 years ago and said of her own country:

It is inevitable that we develop special schools as there is no special educational provision for many disabled children in our country. Then later, we can move to establishing inclusive schools.

From reading papers about India's education system, I know that questions have been asked here too about the conflict between special schools or integrated schools. I should like to say that I was in no doubt 10 years ago, and I am in no doubt now, from a human rights perspective and from the wealth of international, as well as national, experience in favour of inclusive education, the expansion of a segregated special education system for disabled children at this point in history would be utterly wrong. The central issue here is one of membership of the mainstream. Who is eligible for ordinary school and who is not? Behind the change in the international climate of opinion on policy, remarkable things are now happening in ordinary schools in very many different countries, India included. There are two education authorities in Canada (near Toronto) where there are no special schools. All children are in the mainstream. CSIE has reports on this. In London, there is an education authority called Newham, fully committed to inclusion and which is nearing the closure of its last special schools, having transferred hundreds of children, staff, equipment and so on from special schools to the mainstream system.

Moving on from this brief look at four international reports, I now want to turn to America where there has been a recent national study of inclusive education. It was carried out in 1995 by the National Center on Educational Restructuring and Inclusion. Evidence from all 50 states shows that:

- The number of school districts reporting inclusive education programmes has increased significantly since 1994.
- The outcomes for students in inclusive education programmes were positive.
- Teachers participating in such programmes reported positive professional outcomes for themselves.
- Students with a wider range of disabilities than before were now in inclusive programmes.
- School restructuring efforts were having an impact on inclusive education programmes and vice-versa.

The study found that students with all types of disabilities or learning difficulties and at all levels of severity were being included for their education.

In the State of Oregon, the local School District of Ontario said: 'The only criterion for a student to attend any of the schools is that they must be BREATHING!' The type or severity of disability or learning difficulty is not the criteria for membership of the mainstream in that part of America! That School District told the researchers: 'All students with disabilities who live in the school district have the opportunity to be totally included in the regular classroom and the extra-curricular activities of their school.'

Speculating about the future of special educational provision across America, the report concludes that inclusive education must now become fully infused in the work of educational reform. Restructured schools would be the schools where diversity would be valued, and it called for federal and state funding to be reformed to support inclusion.

A report from the European commission in Brussels outlines principles of good practice in combating current systems of discrimination against disabled people, children and adults. In the section dealing with education, the European Commission's Report says:

- Everyone should have equal educational opportunities.
- The aims of education are the same for all learners.
- High quality mainstream education is an entitlement for all.
- Mainstream education systems should be accessible for all pupils. This includes physical access, access to the curriculum, and to all other aspects of school life.

And it endorses the whole-school approach if successful inclusive education is to be a reality.

To summarise, the documents we have looked at help to testify to the strength of international support for inclusion. Of course, none of these documents is the law in any individual country but they have the power to influence policy makers on a wide scale. The documents also contribute significantly to the debate on issues and help with the design of strategies for change.

UK Policy Changes

Coming back to the UK, I have to say that progress with inclusive education in the UK has been in spite of, rather than because of, our education laws. The legal duty to integrate has always been a weak one, ever since it came into force in 1983. The reasons behind this slow but steady movement towards more inclusive education are that parents are demanding it, teachers want to do it, and the local educational and political pressure to change is real in many, though not all, areas of the country. Special school populations are falling but the numbers of children with emotional problems are rising.

It has been a complex and difficult journey and it still is. Not least because of the market forces now in place across the whole of our education system. These forces include: examination league tables, cuts in expenditure and schools controlling their own budget, increased testing at all ages, and semi-independent status for more and more schools. All these government policies have helped to create a negative philosophy of selecting the brightest and isolating the weakest.

There was an important decision last year by our largest teacher union, the National Union of Teachers, which agreed a policy motion supporting the Salamanca Statement. Like anywhere else, the teaching professions in the UK have traditionally seen the long-standing investments in separate special education as something that would remain. Those investments include: teacher training, career structure, buildings and land, belief systems, ethos, and emotional or spiritual commitment.

And until integration, or inclusive education, started to develop, these investments made sense to them. For the NUT (National Union of Teachers) to pass this motion is, truly, a remarkable change in our country and will open up positive avenues for change.

CSIE's evidence is that growing numbers of parents in UK now want their disabled child educated in the mainstream, with appropriate supports, alongside non-disabled brothers and sisters and peer group. Whether from a human rights perspective, or from a personal conviction, they ask the question: 'If it can happen in one town, why can't it happen in another?'

The voice of disabled adults has been important in the inclusion debate, particularly in the United States and Canada, and now in the UK. The British Council of Organisations of Disabled People, representing 7,50,000 disabled people across the UK, recently passed a policy statement saying that:

Placing of disabled children in segregated schools is a discriminatory policy which the Disabled People's Movement can no longer tolerate.

There is not time to talk about another recent world-wide change but it must go on the agenda for future discussions. And that is the internet and inclusive education. The potential for all of us is enormous.

References

United Nations (1993) 'The Standard Rules on the Equalisation of Opportunities for Persons with Disabilities'. New York: UN.

UNESCO (1994) 'Salamanca Statement and Framework for Action on Special Needs Education'. Paris: UNESCO.

UNICEF (1989) 'UN Convention on the Rights of the Child'. New York: UNICEF.

16

Issues at the System and School Level

Seamus Hegarty

A challenge facing countries world-wide is to improve, or establish for the first time, good educational provision for children with disabilities and learning difficulties. (This is a very diverse group and, for convenience, I shall be referring to them as having special educational needs.) It is widely accepted that this provision should be made in ordinary schools to the greatest extent possible. This is for reasons of educational efficacy, efficient use of resources and, above all, human rights. Much has been said and written about these issues, and I do not intend to debate them further here.

What I shall do is outline the issues involved in ensuring that children with special educational needs do receive a good education in ordinary schools. This entails discussion at both policy and practice levels. The topic is a large one and I must necessarily be brief. I shall propose a framework of issues, at system level and at school level, and then discuss the former in some detail.

In doing so, I shall draw on a publication prepared for UNESCO entitled Educating Children and Young People with Disabilities (Hegarty, 1993a). This summarises estimates of the shortfall in appropriate educational provision, sets out the basic underlying principles, details key strategies for policy makers in developing provision and puts forward a framework for use in auditing national practice with regard to special educational provision (Hegarty, 1993a).

System Level

Developments at system level are affected by numerous, interrelated factors. Even in small countries, education systems are complicated structures, which in turn interact with other social, technological and economic structures. School systems operate within a context defined by mass media, the labour market, family structures, religious beliefs, cultural norms and so on. Further, since in a system the component parts are interconnected, it is unlikely that a single element can be changed without affecting many others, perhaps in ways that can be difficult to predict. In a large country like India, where there are a number of administrative levels, these factors multiply in diversity, and understanding the interrelationships between them becomes correspondingly more challenging.

The factors selected for consideration here are key ones and each is important in its own rights, but their full impact can only be understood within an organic system. The seven factors put forward for consideration are:

- Legislation and policy
- Administration
- Educational provision
- Early childhood education
- Professional development
- Parental rights
- Research and development.

Legislation

Legislation is a long way from practical action in schools and classrooms. In a country, however, that rightly prides itself on its commitment to democracy and that can point to major social changes brought about by democratic means, the role of legislation is paramount.

There are more general reasons why legislation is important in improving special educational provision. First, appropriate legislation can articulate and reinforce a country's policy on special education. Educational and social policies are usually more detailed and flexible than any underpinning legislation, but a legal framework can hold the different elements of policy together, clarify ambiguities and resolve tensions among them.

Second, legislation can help secure resources or the appropriate channelling of resources. For example, it can be used to target expenditure on certain groups of pupils, it can mandate administrative structures that facilitate certain types of provision, it can insist on certain levels of teacher training, and of course, it can require that special educational provision be made in ordinary schools.

Third, legislation provides ammunition for those who want to bring about change. Quite simply, if something is mandated and is not happening, those who campaign for change have an extra argument. Take parents' involvement in decisions about their children, for example. In most countries there is a great deal of rhetoric about acknowledging parents' rights, but very often these rights are ignored: parents have no part in the assessment of their child, placement decisions are taken without reference to them, they have very little opportunity to appeal and they have very limited information about or involvement in their child's schooling. But if effective legislation has been passed that guarantees their right to be consulted on their child's assessment and any decisions taken as a consequence, this situation is transformed. They are no longer dependent on the goodwill of professionals and have a proper means of redress when their child's best interests are not being met.

Fourth, legislation can help to change attitudes. What is required by statute has more status than what is optional. A country that regulates special educational provision by legislation confers legitimacy on it and makes it more likely that parents, professionals and the public will view it in a positive way.

As far as I have been able to find out, India does not have extensive legislation covering special educational provision. The Constitution refers to 'provision for...disablement' (Article 41), and various policies on education for all might be understood to imply certain obligations in respect of children with special educational needs. Unless I have misunderstood the situation, however, there is a legislative gap which merits serious attention. It is inappropriate for an outsider to say how this gap should be filled. One has to be aware too of the provenance of legislative statements in different countries, whether these are contained in formal acts of Parliament or in regulations, circulars, notes of guidance and so on. This varies from country to country, and it is seldom possible for an outsider to discern how legislation meshes with other forces for social change in a given country.

What may be helpful is a listing of the range of topics which tend to be covered in special education legislation across countries.

- Basic entitlement, including age range
- Definitions, including categories
- Responsibilities
- Organisation and administration
- Funding
- Identification and assessment
- Provision
  - school types
  - curriculum entitlement
  - integration
  - arrangements within schools
  - preschool and post-school
- Support services
- Monitoring arrangements
- Teacher education
- Parents

Administration

Administration and the organisation of special education raise particular problems. These stem from the multiplicity of tasks to be carried out, the dispersion of responsibility for them and, in many countries, the diversity of funding sources. Special education extends beyond education into health, social welfare and rehabilitation. Along with teachers, it involves psychologists, health workers and therapists.

The education ministry is responsible for educating pupils with disabilities in most countries. The most common arrangement is to have within the Ministry of Education a separate department dealing with special education. Generally, the special education system runs parallel to the mainstream system, with modifications as judged necessary, and the function of the special education department is to provide administrative support for this parallel system. In some cases, special education is subsumed under the department dealing with primary education.

The importance of appropriate administrative support is twofold: it shapes the nature of the provision made, and provides the co-ordination that is necessary.

The impact of administrative arrangements on the nature of provision can be seen clearly in relation to integration. When special education is administered quite separately from the general education system, it is difficult to achieve much integration at the level of practice. Even if the policy is in favour of integration, the separation of funding, teacher supply and curriculum entailed by separate administrative arrangements places major obstacles in the way of implementing the policy. The co-ordinating functions of administration are wide-ranging where special education is concerned. They encompass planning, resource allocation, supply and training of personnel, buildings, materials and transport as well as co-ordination of the different service elements. In many countries these functions entail co-ordination structures at national, regional and local levels.

Special Educational Provision

Pupils with special educational needs are a very diverse group and their educational requirements are no less varied. Some need a highly structured environment with considerable individual attention, others benefit from access to sophisticated equipment or specialist staff, while yet others need little more than minor adjustments to normal schooling. The response of education systems around the world to the educational needs of these pupils has been to establish many different kinds of special educational provision, ranging from segregated special schools to fully integrated provision in ordinary schools. This range is often described in terms of a rough continuum so far as the education and experience of the individual pupil is concerned:

1. full-time placement in special school;
2. part-time in special school, part-time in ordinary school;
3. full-time placement in a unit or special class;
4. part-time in special class, part-time in ordinary class;
5. placement in ordinary class, withdrawal for specialist work;
6. placement in ordinary class, in-class support; and
7. placement in fully integrated class.

The actual pattern of special educational provision varies a good deal because of local circumstances and traditions, but also because special education is not sufficiently developed to permit precise matching of pupil needs to organisational arrangement. For that reason alone it is probably beneficial to have available a variety of organisational arrangements: pupils with special needs are more likely to receive appropriate education if special educational provision of many kinds is on offer. A variety of local situations is a further argument for diverse provision: it is necessary to be flexible to capitalise on available resources and to respond to individual needs.

While diversity of provision is generally desirable, there is need of a coherent framework that integrates the different elements into a unified whole and relates special educational provision to the educational provision made for all pupils. A framework for special educational provision has to encompass numerous dimensions, setting out norms and guidance for practice in respect of each and drawing attention to the interconnections between them. The following are among the dimensions to be considered:

- admission and exit criteria
- staffing
- curriculum and assessment
- physical environment
- financing
- parents
- relationship to mainstream provision
- external support.

Early Childhood Education

Experience in a wide variety of settings has shown the importance of early childhood education. The absence of appropriate stimulation in infancy and early childhood ranks alongside malnutrition and poverty as a major source of disadvantage and retarded development. This is true of all children but is especially true of children with disabilities. If sensory perception is impaired, for instance, enhanced stimulation is required to compensate for it, but frequently what is offered is even less stimulation, not more. Indeed, the interruption of normal patterns of development arising from the disability is often more handicapping for the child than the direct consequences of the disability itself.

For these reasons early childhood education is particularly important for infants with disabilities. National authorities have a significant part to play, both in making the provision and in supporting parents. Parents are the main educators of their children in the earliest years, and a major task for official agencies is to support parents in promoting the development of their young children with disabilities. This can take various forms: material support in dealing with practical problems, training in specific skills, and personal support and counselling. It is also very important to give them a significant role in the conduct of assessment.

The nature of appropriate provision will depend on the local context and resources but should encompass arrangements for identifying children with disabilities as early as possible, assessment to establish what developmental and educational difficulties they may face; and organised preschool education.

Any such provision must be guided by a number of considerations. First, the position of parents is central and every effort should be made to involve them in both the management and the day-to-day running of provision. Second, it is not necessary or even advisable for all preschool provision to be organised by the official authorities. Much provision, especially playgroups and opportunity groups, is effectively organised at local levels by parents or other community groups. Third, preschool provision of every kind for children with disabilities should include children without disabilities. General preschool provision should encompass children with disabilities as a matter of course, and in an ideal world that has adequate preschool provision for all children there would be no need of special arrangements for those with disabilities. Given the paucity of provision and the latter's overwhelming need of it, special arrangements do have to be made and it is important that these allow maximum interaction between children with disabilities and their peers.

Fourth, particular efforts may need to be made where children with disabilities living in rural areas are concerned. The services and professional support that are provided in centres of population may be less available, and community-led initiatives are likely to play a major role. It is incumbent on national and regional authorities to recognise the particular problems experienced by these children and their families and to find ways of stimulating and supporting appropriate community activity.

Professional Development

Developments in special educational provision are critically dependent upon the quality of teaching available. This in turn depends on the opportunities for training and professional development open to teachers.

Teacher education, particularly in-service education, takes on extra significance at a time of change. When conceptualisations of handicap are being revised and integration means that teachers in ordinary schools are expected to teach pupils with special educational needs, training that was previously adequate may need to be supplemented or restructured. This represents a particular challenge in countries where, to begin with, basic teacher education is limited.

A national strategy for teacher education has to start with initial training. A major objective for all countries should be to ensure that all intending teachers learn something about disabilities and be aware of some of their educational implications. They would not become experts in teaching pupils with special needs but they would learn how to modify the curriculum content and teaching approach of the ordinary classroom so as to give access to substantial numbers of pupils with special needs. They would acquire some skills in identifying and assessing pupils with disabilities. They would appreciate the importance of working with parents and would develop appropriate skills. They would also know where their own competence stopped and how they could benefit from collaborating with specialists.

A national strategy should also make provision for in-service education for classroom teachers and headteachers on matters relating to special educational needs. This can be provided in a great variety of ways. At the most basic level, general awareness courses can be provided for individual teachers or, more usefully, for all the staff in a school. The latter can be arranged quite economically by occasional training days when the staff come together without pupils. More substantial training can be provided by arranging for individual staff members to go on appropriate courses.

Classroom assistants can play a major role in the education of pupils with special needs, in both special schools and ordinary schools. They can carry out a wide range of functions: providing physical care, acting as paraprofessionals to implement therapy programmes drawn up by professionals, and contributing to pupils' education under the teacher's instruction. Appropriate training is necessary if classroom assistants are to be used to maximum advantage. People recruited to work as classroom assistants frequently have had no prior training; if they have had any, it is likely to be in general childcare. In-service training is therefore required. This can take the form of on-the-job instruction or formal courses for which an appropriate time allocation is made.

There are many professionals who can be involved in educating pupils with special needs—teachers, psychologists, therapists, social workers, doctors and paramedical staff. In practice, they frequently work in isolation from each other. This arises in part from the fact that different professional groups bring their own perspectives and skills to the task and do not have adequate appreciation of the perspectives and skills of their colleagues. Appropriate training can help to ensure that they come to a better understanding of each other's roles and competencies. This can be achieved in the fullest form by means of joint training, whereby members of different professional groups have elements of their initial training in common or share in-service training courses. Another approach is to include in the training of a given group specific inputs on the roles of colleagues from other professional groups. Formal training is not always necessary: when different professionals do have occasion to work together, appropriate attitudes and ways of working can do much to build up a common set of understandings.

Parental Rights

Parents are the child's first and natural teachers, and it is incumbent on the state to help them discharge this role to the best of their ability. Parents of children with special educational needs can play a major role in their education—if helped and allowed to. This can include assisting in school activities, contributing to assessment and curriculum planning, implementing programmes at home and monitoring progress.

This role is first and foremost a matter of principle: parents have the right to be involved in their children's education. This entails rights in respect of assessment, decisions on where the child is to be educated, and the organisation and content of the educational provision made. For young children with special educational needs, parental rights are of the utmost importance. Parents' right to be present when their child is assessed should be formally recognised. Parents should have access to the information on which assessment outcomes are based and they should be told what the outcome is as soon as possible. Parents can make a substantive contribution to the assessment process—they after all are the ones who know the child best—and it is good practice to systematise parental input in this way.

Research and Development

Educating pupils with special needs is a complex matter. It is likely to be significantly improved if it based on good information about the nature of these pupils' learning needs and how best to meet them. Four broad areas of relevant R&D activity can be identified:

1. Studies designed to separate different forms of disability, deepen understanding of them and clarify their educational implications. These should draw on a variety of areas of study—medical, psychological and sociological as well as education.
2. Incidence surveys to establish the extent of local need.
3. Development activities directed at curricula, teaching approaches and the deployment of resources. This is a very broad area, including activities as diverse as developing sign languages, devising individual learning programmes and mobilising community resources for educational purposes.
4. Evaluation: This too is exceedingly broad but also quite essential. Educational programmes, particularly at a time of change, must be monitored to make sure that they are achieving their objectives and that resources are being used to maximum beneficial effect.

R&D expenditure may be deemed an expendable luxury when service budgets are severely constrained. This would be unfortunate, however, because relatively modest expenditure can secure much more efficient targeting of the available resources. Much can be learned too by means of efficient information exchange. No less important than maintaining an R&D capacity to service local needs is an efficient means of exchanging information with other countries and capitalising on their experience.

School Level

If we turn to the school level, the central issue has to do with school reform. Integration is not a matter of placing individual pupils with disabilities in an ordinary school, perhaps making a few minor changes and hoping that everything works out. The reason special schools have been necessary is that ordinary schools have not been able or willing to educate pupils with special educational needs. In fact, many ordinary schools fail to provide appropriate education for large numbers of other children.

So the task is one of school reform, of creating schools which provide appropriate education to the widest possible range of pupils, not just those of average and above average ability. The creation of such schools is governed, of course, by many of the system level factors referred to above. It is important to have a vision of what such a 'school for all', as our Scandinavian colleagues call it, looks like. This has been spelled out in numerous publications, including, for example, Hegarty (1993b). The requisite changes can usefully be described in terms of seven headings:

- *Curriculum:* What is taught, with particular reference to establishing a balance between offering a mainstream curriculum framework and taking account of individual needs.
- *Pedagogy:* How it is taught, again with reference to providing specialist support without isolating pupils from peers.
- *Academic organisation:* How the school organises itself to deliver the curriculum effectively to the widest possible range of pupils, by means of appropriate pupil grouping, arrangements for supplementary teaching and timetable construction.
- *Staffing:* Teachers, classroom assistants and support staff, all to be deployed flexibly, but with a shared dynamic focus on achieving a 'school for all'.
- *Professional development:* Essential underpinning of any school reform, to encompass attitude change, increased understanding and skill development.
- *Parental involvement:* Collaboration to include sharing of information, involvement in curriculum delivery, parent support and liaison with professional agencies.
- *External support:* Special schools and support agencies to provide essential input—training, assessment, curriculum planning, therapy —but without usurping the school's principal responsibility.

The task facing us is formidable. Success will not be achieved easily. There are few more important challenges facing our education systems, however. No society can be regarded as truly civilised if it ignores its less advantaged citizens or treats them less favourably in educational terms. It is for us to rise to the challenge, to commit ourselves to a vision of one school for all, and to do all in our power to create such schools the length and breadth of the land.

References

Hegarty, S. (1993a) *Educating Children and Young People with Disabilities: Principles and the Review of Practice.* Paris: UNESCO.
—— (1993b) *Meeting Special Needs in Ordinary Schools: An Overview.* London: Cassell.

17

Three Decades of Integrated Education

Karl–Gustaf Stukat

I will begin with a few glimpses of the changes over time that have taken place in my country, Sweden, with respect to the educational situation of disabled children. This account will be based on personal experiences, but I believe that they fairly well reflect the general development.

The pupils of the classes I attended myself as a school boy in the 1930s were a very mixed sample. Some boys had reading and writing difficulties, some a more general learning disability, others did not see or hear well, and social or even delinquent behaviour was not uncommon. No doubt most of these children would nowadays be considered to be in need of special educational support. But then not much of such support was available. Repeating grades was the standard treatment for school failure. This period of what might be called 'primitive integration' was basically a period of neglect. Exceptions from this pattern were the special institutions for blind, deaf and mentally retarded children which had been established in the nineteenth century, and a limited number of remedial classes for slow learners in the larger cities.

As a young teacher in the 1940s, I taught in special classes of this kind, which were now growing rapidly in number, as were also other types of special classes for children with specific disabilities, e.g., reading, hearing, sight, speech and social-emotional difficulties. There was the double argument for this expansion that special classes would offer appropriate education for disabled children and at the same time relieve regular classes from, I quote, 'the burdensome deadweight that only slows down the speed'.

In the process of selecting children for special education, testing played an important role. Most of the tests were called 'diagnostic' and they could be used for diagnostic purposes, but most often their main function was to select children for special classes or schools. I worked for some time at a school psychology office, and a considerable part of my working time consisted of talking to parents and teachers and testing children in order to gather information upon which placement and other advice could be based.

The curriculum of the special classes varied locally. Typically it was a simplified version of the regular curriculum, but with stronger emphasis on individual adaptation of aims, methods and materials. Other features were understanding rather than moralistic attitudes to a pupil's school difficulties, close contacts with the parents and co-operation with social welfare. In this way the early phases of special education can be seen as a forerunner to progressive ideas and practice that reached general education later. This conviction led me to write an article which concluded that special education may be defined as education desirable for all children.

The expansion of the special classes continued with increased speed through the 1950s and part of the 1960s. This was in a way paradoxical, since the Parliament and the national committees that were in this period busy with reforming the Swedish school system, very strongly stated that the compulsory school should be comprehensive in the sense of being non-streamed. Necessary individualisation was expected to take place within the framework of the school class. When I once asked one of the most prominent school reformers why the general principle of comprehensiveness was not applied also to disabled pupils, he answered something like 'they are a deviant group'. And I think that was a rather representative opinion of the time.

New signals came, however, from two directions: ideology and research. For me the latter was first apparent. International research as well as our own studies suggested that the assumed beneficial effects of special class or special school attendance for disabled children were doubtful. Comparisons between equivalent groups of disabled pupils in regular and special classes or schools did not demonstrate better school achievement or adjustment in the special settings—with respect to learning results, the tendency was rather the opposite. It was this body of research that gave rise to the often cited challenging question: What is special about special education?

The impact of empirical research was, however, less striking than the influence from the ideological arguments for equality that were strongly articulated during the same time. In Scandinavia these arguments were first expressed in terms of 'normalisation' and later as 'integration' or 'inclusion'.

The changes in educational practice that have taken place during the last 30 years can be sketched as follows. The large group of pupils with moderate disabilities who were earlier placed in special classes have successively moved into regular classes. A first step in this direction was taken with the introduction of remedial clinics attached to the schools. Pupils in need of extra support could go to these clinics a few hours a week and receive remedial instruction and other help from a special teacher. This model was modified in another arrangement called 'co-ordinated special education'. Here the special teacher comes into the regular class and works with one or more pupils with difficulties. The assumption is that this help is given under close co-operation between the teacher and the special teacher working side by side. It was often found, however, that little such co-operation takes place. Another critical factor seems to be the teachers' conception of what should be the aims of the special support. In an interview study we asked teachers about this. The most frequent answers were: 'so that the pupil can follow the class', 'so that he will not be too far behind' and similar formulations. This norm-oriented view (which is also apparent in the school's grading system) is discrepant with the individual need orientation underlying integration ideology as it was, for example, expressed in the national curriculum: 'Children are different when they come to school. Neither should the school endeavour to make them alike', with the addition: 'The school has a particular responsibility for children with difficulties and children who belong to minorities. Therefore it cannot give an equal amount of assistance. It must especially, and in cooperation with others, give support to those who by different reasons are in need of help.'

As can be seen from this quotation, strong emphasis is laid upon the school's responsibility. This emphasis is well expressed in the pointed formulation: 'Pupils with learning difficulties can be seen as a school with teaching difficulties.' An arrangement for increasing the school's potential to handle special needs problems within the regular setting, which is practised to a growing extent, is to form team units with four or five teachers, one of whom is a special teacher. If this teamwork proceeds in a co-operative spirit, the conditions for flexibility are no doubt improved.

The inclusion of disabled children in regular classes has meant an increase in the variation among pupils. It has meant a challenge for the teachers—and for many, not an easy one—to try new and flexible methods to meet individual needs. Not seldom it has become an important task for the special teacher to advise and assist the regular teachers in this work. Thus, in addition to giving remedial support to pupils, the role of the special teacher (or 'special pedagogue' as is the more common name now) includes the function to be an 'agent of innovation' in the school.

The experiences described refer mainly to the integration of pupils with moderate learning difficulties. The situation is somewhat more complex with respect to children with other kinds and degrees of handicaps. Physically disabled children to a large extent (90 per cent) attend regular classes, those who are neither severely disabled nor have multiple impairments, as can be the case for children with cerebral palsy and spina bifida. Some features of physically disabled pupils' situations in an integrated setting are described in the following way in a Swedish questionnaire and interview study. About half of the pupils were reported to need practical help during the lessons, for example, with moving in the class, handling exercise books and ruler, handwriting, etc. Outside the classroom, most need for help was related to meals and toileting. For about 60 per cent of the pupils, adaptations of the school building were judged to be needed, and in most schools this need has been met, although sometimes only partially. Technical aids used were specially designed chairs and tables, electric typewriters, non-slip table-plates, special rulers and pencils with adapted holders. The study goes back some years; today computers would be added to the list.

Of interest in this study is also an analysis that was made of pupils (17 out of 200) for whom integration had not worked well, which led to removal of the pupils into special classes. Certain patterns appeared as to the reasons behind the transfer—conflict relating to peers and teachers, insufficient resources for remedial instruction, teacher insecurity in coping with disability problems, etc. The most frequent single factor behind the pupils' removal was inability to meet achievement standards. All but one had difficulties in this respect. The learning difficulties were often combined with aggression, affective outbursts, isolation or passivity. Typically, the learning and social-emotional problems had developed into a vicious circle which gradually made the situation untenable. In this process the physical disability by itself seemed to play a relatively minor role. A few pupils complained about being teased because of their physical impairment, but the general attitude of the peers was one of tolerance, more seldom of close contact. A main conclusion from the study was that the placing of a disabled child in a regular class does not automatically guarantee successful integration. Among the prerequisites discussed were: co-operative planning by the teacher, special teacher, parents, involving the pupil, preparing the pupil and the class for integration, and setting up realistic goals adapted to the pupil's needs and capacities. The importance of pre- and in-service teacher training in special needs education was also stressed.

Also blind and sight impaired children are nowadays to a high degree integrated in regular classes. The change has been quite rapid. Not long ago most blind children were placed in Tomteboda, a special boarding school common to the whole country, and those with substantially lowered vision in so-called 'sight classes'. Ten years ago the special school was closed and also the sight classes were abolished. The Tomteboda institute has been transformed into a resource centre to which teachers, pupils, parents and others concerned can come for information and training. The centre is also responsible for research and developing aids. The blind and sight disabled pupils in regular class are usually helped by an assistant, and both pupils and teachers receive support and advice from a visiting consultant, and in most schools also from a special teacher.

There have been careful studies made of blind children who have been followed from preschool into school years. Observations from these studies, among other things, indicate that the blind child's adjustment to the group life in preschool is dependent upon an adequate level of language skills, and that the introduction to a larger group sometimes comes too early. In school, teacher efforts are usually too narrowly focused on improving the blind child's cognitive skills, and in special training courses teaching methods and techniques are often given the main attention. But the studies convincingly show that it is social and emotional problems— lack of friends, of belongingness, of appreciation—that worry the children most. These concerns become especially serious in adolescent years. Experiences of this kind demonstrate the need for a holistic educational approach.

The educational situation of hearing impaired children has been the object of much, often heated, debate through the years. Experiences of integrating children who mainly rely on sign language for their communication have often been discouraging. As a consequence, deaf and profoundly hearing impaired children receive their education in special schools. A majority (three-quarters) of hearing disabled children go to regular schools. Those with a moderate hearing loss that permits lip reading, but makes communication in groups awkward, usually attend their own unit within these schools but share some activities with hearing pupils. Most hearing impaired children belong to regular classes. Criteria for this placement are that the pupil can follow the instruction with the help of technical aids and, if necessary, support from an itinerant specialist teacher who is also an adviser of the school staff. Extensive observation studies have shown that hearing impaired pupils in regular classes often struggle with social as well as learning problems which are often overlooked by the teacher.

The group of disabled pupils whose education has attracted most discussion and trial of practical alternatives of integration is probably the mentally retarded. First, I should mention that in my country fewer children of school age (1 per cent) are being registered as mentally retarded than is international practice. It means that a large number of children who would be classed as mentally retarded in other countries belong to regular classes in Sweden. For the pupils, the general educational support system that I have described earlier is available. As to those registered, 5 per cent are in special schools and 95 per cent in regular schools. The retarded pupils in regular schools, as a rule, form their own class units, while a minority (10 per cent) attend regular classes. Much exploratory work is going on in schools to find ways of encouraging interaction between the mentally retarded children and their schoolmates. In many cases, a combination of group and individual integration is practised.

As an example of this approach can be mentioned an activity that has taken place during the whole 9-year period of compulsory school in a local community. It started with a first grade class of 26 pupils, four of whom were registered as mentally retarded and who represented different degrees of retardation. The four sometimes worked in the Big Group (as it was called) and sometimes formed their own Little Group. The conditions were favourable insofar as the school administration and the staff—a regular teacher with support from a special teacher—were concerned and the parents were also positive to the arrangement, the latter using their legal right to choose the school form for their children. Ample time was devoted to planning, both long range and short range. Individualised basic skill training was combined with co-operative work within and outside the classroom. Art, music, handicraft and physical exercise took place in the Big Group and gave opportunities for solo or group performances. The evaluations that have been made reflect varying but mainly favourable responses from the pupils, parents and teachers. It is interesting to note that several parents of the non-disabled pupils stressed the advantage that their children had learnt a valuable understanding of individual differences. An observation that has also been made in other similar projects was that problems tend to increase on the secondary level as achievement norms become more prominent and the youngsters go into a sensitive period of personality development. It should be mentioned that the experiences from this project are now utilised in a new project beginning at the start of school. Among other things, 'seniors' from the former Little Group function as resource persons for the beginners.

After this general survey of the situation and development of integration in Sweden, I will now focus on some prominent issues that have been much discussed. One such topic has concerned the true meaning of integration. To begin with, the new ideas were brought forward under the name of 'normalisation', usually meaning that the conditions of education—and of society at large—should be changed so as to further equality and full participation of disabled people. But the term sometimes came to be associated with 'norms' and to the possible meaning of 'making disabled people normal', which is probably the reason why 'integration' has become the more common word, at least in the educational context.

During one period, the main discourse was about such concepts as physical, functional and social integration, ending in a general agreement that being physically together is not enough, but is only a prerequisite of integration in a deeper sense. In the current discussion, the focus is not so much on integration in the narrow sense of moving a disabled pupil into the regular school or class as on the school itself and its potential to care for the needs of the whole spectrum of children. In a way, this means a shift of perspective from integration to problems of creating a non-segregated school for all. One way to mark this shift is the use of the new term 'inclusion' and an 'inclusive school'. But change of terms is not the essential thing. In order to have a real impact, qualitative changes must take place in school. Otherwise, there is a risk that 'a school for all' will mean a return to what I have earlier described as 'primitive integration'.

The policy of an inclusive school is a radical challenge to teacher training, pre-service as well as in-service. As a consequence, new programmes have been developed to prepare teachers and other staff for the new tasks. For a few years there have been ten units, equivalent to ten weeks, of special needs education included in the general pre-service teacher training programme. It is spread over the whole 3½ to 4 years of training, and different special needs aspects are incorporated into different courses and practice periods, e.g., ideological and social bases of education, developmental psychology, individual differences, learning, curriculum and instructional. It is interesting to note that a very similar Indian model is described by Professor Jangira (1995) in a article in Prospects, the UNESCO quarterly review of comparative education.

Another similarity is that in both cases an optional course is also offered. The Swedish ten units course has a common part, 'special needs education in school and society', aimed at helping students to develop a conscious and personal perspective on the concept of 'a non-segregated school for all'. Another part of the course is devoted to in-depth study by application of the general principles in a chosen area, such as learning disabilities, social-emotional problems, etc. This optional course has become very popular among the students; at our university, it is at present chosen by more than half of the students. One reason for its popularity may be that it is known that those who have taken it stand a good chance of being hired as teachers after their certification.

The former special teacher training programme has now been revised into a 1½ year programme for 'special pedagogues', available not only for persons with a teacher certificate, but also for people with other university training. The change of name and broadened recruitment reflect the intention that these professionals should work as consultants rather than as teachers. They are expected to identify the needs for special provision at their school, help teachers in planning their instruction so as to meet also the needs of disabled pupils and generally function as innovators, 'agents of change'. They are also expected to initiate in-service courses of special education for ordinary teachers. There is a strong need for action of this kind. There is no national in-service programme; in the currently highly decentralised Swedish system, the local communities or even the local schools are responsible for in-service activities, which means great variation across the country.

A question that is often raised is: What are the effects of integration in a longer and broader perspective? In spite of the rather extensive period of integration policy and practice, there is a relative lack of studies of its long-term impact. Some research is, however, beginning to appear. I will mention an interesting recent study about 'the first integration generation'. It built on close contact during 3 years with ten mentally retarded young adults.

The young people spoke openly about their difficulties, but it was also striking that they insisted on their rights to get support from the society. Their arguments were often drawn from official integration rhetoric. A pattern of 'integration culture' was discernible, represented by the disabled themselves, their close network (parents, mates) and professionals embracing the integration ideology. The reasoning of the young and their core group sometimes reflected conflicts between this subculture and a more competitive majority culture. This was, for example, illustrated in a talk about differences and similarities among people with the mother of a retarded daughter. The mother denied that her daughter differed from other young people with respect to capacity to profit from education in an ordinary school, having a job, becoming a mother, etc. At the same time she was very eager to emphasise her daughter's right to the support, e.g., employment with salary subsidies, that she could get because of her disability.

In a theoretical context, the subculture can be interpreted as a social strategy which the disabled of the first integration generation have developed together with relatives and professionals for handling the stigma they risk being exposed to in the majority society. A current issue with respect to this welfare and benefactor based culture is that it is brought about at the price of reduced personal autonomy. That it is not necessarily so I could see with my own eyes the other night from a TV show, where a stand-up comedian with severe cerebral palsy, with excellent skills, exploited his disability as a fool's mirror for the audience to discover their stereotypical attitudes and beliefs. This actor probably contributed more to the understanding of a disability—and of oneself—than any professor in the handicap field could have done.

References

Andersson, B. (1996) 'Integrering i särskolan' (Integration of Mentally Retarded Pupils), in T. Rabe and A. Hill (eds) *Boken om integrering*. Corona: Malmö.

Emanuelsson, I. (1996) 'Integrering—bevarad normal variation i olikheter' (Integration—Keeping Normal Variation in Differences), in T. Rabe and A. Hill (eds) *Boken om integrering*. Corona: Malmö.

Gustavsson, A. (1996) 'Integrering som motkultur—erfarenheter från den första integreringsgenerationen' (Integration as an Alternative Culture—Experiences from the First Generation of Integration), in T. Rabe and A. Hill (eds) *Boken om integrering*. Corona: Malmö.

Läroplan för grundskolan (1980) (National Swedish Curriculum for the Comprehensive School).

Paulsson, K. (1980) 'Analys av varför integrering av rh-elever i vanlig klass ibland "misslyckas" (Analysis of Why Integration of Pupils with Motor Disability Sometimes is "A Failure")'. Report no. 95, Department of Practical Education, University of Gothenburg, Sweden.

Stukat, K-G. (1983) 'Lärares uppofattningar om specialundervisningens mål' (Teacher Conceptions of the Aims of Special Education). Seminar paper, Department of Education, University of Gothenburg, Sweden.

18

Integration to Inclusion: Change of Paradigm from the Danish Experience

Peter Gam Henriksen

Danish efforts concerning integration have their roots in the school policy debates of the 1940s and the 1950s, which gradually created a political majority for the belief that the differentiation of students after a test in the fifth form had lifelong consequences for the students. Indeed, it meant that their future social situation was already determined. This debate later split up into two movements, the movement for a comprehensive school and the movement for a school for everyone. Both of these had integration as their main aim.

The Comprehensive School

This movement wanted the implementation of the comprehensive school and, in a broader sense, the integration/inclusion—or, more correctly, the non-segregation—of all students regardless of ability.

In 1958, an amendment of the law for the primary school was passed, according to which schools were not allowed to divide students in the first seven years of schooling, and in 1975, the Primary Act on the Folkeskole in principle established a comprehensive basic school from the first to the tenth form. In the same period, however, and until about 10 years ago, the number of support lessons spent on special education increased quite a lot, and these lessons were mainly special arrangements outside the classroom in so-called clinics at the school.

As the Danish educator and politician, Finn Held, put it: 'We didn't suppress the division of school. It is now turning up in another design.' This paradoxical incompatibility between, on the one hand, the principal agreement on the aim, 'being willing to integrate even more in general education', and, on the other hand, the actual increasing segregation of students and teaching inside and outside the ordinary classroom has been the focus of the debate on integration in Denmark. Whereas formerly the school system concentrated on the learning difficulties of students, attention now has increasingly turned to the conditions which to a large extent create difficulties for students.

This point of view is reflected in the recent legislation. For instance, in the Government Notice on Special Education, it is pointed out that 'it lies with every teacher to plan and to carry out his teaching with so much differentiation that to the greatest possible extent it accommodates those differences in learning conditions which the students are having' (MoE, 1990). In 1993 a new law for the primary school was passed. In this law the demand for differentiation in teaching has also been stressed (Primary Education Act, 1993).

As the idea of a common norm applied to all students in school seems to have been abandoned, a parallel shift in teacher work becomes possible. Instead of seeking out and naming student learning differences and deficits, teachers from now on shall focus on creating and tailoring the curriculum so that schooling in fact is working for every student.

The School for Everyone

The debate about the comprehensive school in the 1940s was mainly about children who had mild special education needs, but it formed the basis of subsequent debates about the schooling of children with more serious learning difficulties and other handicaps. In the Law of 1959, about the Care of the Mentally Deficient, the right to education was specified for every child, and as a consequence the 'School for Everyone' movement arose.

All children with severe disabilities and handicaps were from then on considered educable and had the right to demand a meaningful education.

The care needs of pupils were to be met within an adaptive learning environment. The principle that 'the teaching of handicapped students should be broadened in such way that the children could be taught in an ordinary school system', as formulated in the Parliamentary Resolution, at the same time implied four further principles, which became the guidelines for local authorities:

1. The principle of proximity: Assistance to a handicapped child must be offered as close to the child's home and school as possible.
2. The principle of minimum interference: A child should not receive any more help than is necessary in order to overcome his or her handicap or its consequences.
3. The principle of efficiency: The situations prepared for the child must be worked out in such a way that a handicap can be surmounted and/or its consequences eliminated.
4. The principle of integration/inclusion: All human beings are equal and have the same right to full participation, and everyone should have the chance to become an important and valued member of the community.

These ideas were breaking new ground and were founded on the basic principles of integration, normalisation and decentralisation. Previously a handicap was seen as an individual defect, which could not be helped. Contrary to this, the new point of view stressed that a handicap was in some way related to the environment and therefore amenable to action. According to this perspective, one must act on the basis of a concept of equality which implies that disabled persons—to be set equal—have to be treated differently.

The new ideas of the 1960s and the 1970s were embedded in a period of social and economic growth. Implementation during the 1980s faced economic setbacks, and the ideas on decentralising the care of handicapped children were reduced to just an administrative reform. In January 1980, the legislation related to the primary school was modified, leading to a division of responsibilities between the municipalities and the counties. In future the municipalities had to support students with moderate social and learning difficulties, while the counties were responsible for students with more severe disabilities. The combined effects of the principles of administrative decentralisation and legal normalisation meant that the processes of integration and inclusion were determined locally. There is no direct legislation on integration, only guidelines.

By making a point of administrative decentralisation it became more and more a matter of physical integration in so-called 'normal' environments—on the assumption that social integration was certain to occur. It implied that individual integrated students were allocated a number of support lessons but in addition had to adapt to ordinary/ mainstream education. It was rarely a matter of mainstream schools trying to adapt to the needs and backgrounds of these children. Consequently, it depended entirely on the individual student and teacher whether integration succeeded or failed.

Status of Integration of Handicapped Pupils in Danish Folkeskole

According to reports from the Danish Ministry of Education referring to the Helios Resolution of the European Union in May 1990, the degree of integration of handicapped pupils has reached a level hardly matched by any other country, since only 0.5 per cent of students in primary and lower secondary schools were being educated outside an ordinary school environment.

Viewed as physical integration, there is good reason for Danish satisfaction, but if the intention is that physical integration should be experienced as meaningful for everyone, more qualitative research is needed before such a conclusion can be supported.

Danish Research into Integration

In the late 1980s, Danish research into integration started, ending in 1990. A four-phase research programme was carried out by researchers from RDIER (Royal Danish Institute of Educational Research) and RDSED (Royal Danish School of Educational Studies). The quantitative data below are based on enrolments in the year 1977/78. The main conclusions were:

- Number of students recorded as having severe learning disabilities has been constant.
- Seventy per cent have been taught in county special schools.
- Most of the individually integrated students have been wholly or partly segregated from several teaching areas.

- The process of integration falls apart as students grow older, dropping suddenly after seventh form. More suitable schooling is recommended after seventh form.

In the second part of the research, interviews indicate that the process of integration in schools often has an accidental character, and the practical work of including a student, which should be a corporate responsibility of the school, has been left up to individual teachers.

- While teachers are positive about the internal co-operation taking place within classes, they express discontent in relation to the other teachers in the school, school psychologists, administrators and the staff of the youth centres.
- The general tendency is that the further away from the classroom, the less co-operation there is, and the poorer its quality.

In the third part of the research, parents were interviewed. As few mentioned teasing; it appears that children with disabilities were not being teased in school; but relationships developed in schools seemed not to develop into friendships outside of school. Also many parents said that they felt they had no real choice regarding the selection of school for their child with disabilities.

The Decentralised Strategy of Development

No doubt, we in Denmark have had the best intentions, but why have they been so difficult to carry out?

An answer could be that, although since 1996 we have had a socially formulated ambition of integrating students with disabilities in order to carry out the efforts of integration, we have left implementation to the municipalities and indeed to individual teachers.

For a strategy of development it is of the greatest importance that the experiences are gathered, linked to and disseminated through an institutional network or organisation. Changes of practice (or habitus, in the term used by the French sociologist Bordieu) are bound to institutions and institutional behaviour. If they are practised by single teachers in small 'islands' only, they will not have much impact on developments.

Special Education Projects

In 1988/89 a general primary education programme was launched in Denmark. One hundred million Dkr was allotted over a five-year period. The programme was leading up to a revision of the primary curriculum. Out of some 400 projects, only 10 projects were concerned with integration/inclusion; of these just one entailed complete integration defined by:

- students following the same schedule,
- in the same classrooms, and
- with the same teachers.

Normally, the inclusion of students took place for short periods only, working with special themes or in certain subjects for two or four hours weekly.

In one case, Madeskovskolen in Nakskov, the conditions for complete integration were fulfilled. The project went on for nine years and received the status of being a pilot project under the Folkeskolens Development Council. The educational practice of this project was based on the understanding that handicap is relative and is determined, among other things, by local planning and implementation of education.

The building stones of the project have been:

- Coherent organisation of education as regards subjects and lessons.
- Alternation between courses with differentiated curriculum material specifically related to subjects and cross-curricular activities.
- Workshops which are based on the experiences of the students and on autonomy.
- Daily class meetings and conflict resolution.
- Organisation of the two classrooms to make various activities for various groups possible at the same time.

The principles and conditions of the project have been as follows:

- The special class was taught with an ordinary class of the same age.
- The maximum size of the class was 20 students, of whom three to four belonged to the special class. There were also three to four

students in the ordinary class who had some minor learning difficulties.

- The teacher-team consisted of three teachers, one of whom had a special education background.
- The timetabling and organisation of lessons made it possible for two teachers to be present at the same time.
- Both the students of the special class and the students of the ordinary class followed the curriculum approved by the municipality of Nakskov.

What is remarkable about this project is that it has, throughout nine years of schooling, succeeded in creating a school life which has included both students with disabilities and mainstream students. In a survey in the seventh form, by far the greater part of the so-called 'normal' students said that peer relationships and friendships in the class were good, while most of the students with SEN considered they were very good.

The findings of this successful pilot can be summarised as follows:

Only in a group in which the student or pupil with special education need (SEN) or a disability is able to establish mutual educational relations, is getting linguistic stimulation and has good opportunities for communication, help with his individual development, is able to feel well, secure and accepted and feel that he belongs, can the person concerned be said to be integrated.

Conceptual Aid to Research and Development—Looking Forward

The American researcher Dianne Ferguson raises the question about students with special educational needs: Are they *in* or *of* the class? The question is important for reflection on which kind of integration is desirable and/or achievable. To be *in* a class is but a physical position; to be *of* a class is being a member of a community, to share experiences, work and life.

For Paulo Freire the case is clear. He reaches the conclusion in his theoretical works that 'a (co-operatively) integrated person' is 'a person as object'. I do think most teachers who have worked for the integration of a single student in a 'normal' class will recognise the danger, but also how easily one can treat a pupil as a case a person as an object.

The Danish psychologist Ivy Schousbo operates with four different kinds of integration:

1. Co-operative integration: The established social unit and the teachers co-operate in deciding aims for the integration, because it was never decided in advance. This seems to be the exception.
2. Assimilation: The integration of a single student in an ordinary class.
3. Fragmentary: The integration of a group of students in an ordinary class, mostly only for limited periods of time, in a few selected subjects.
4. Formal: The integration often carried out by politicians and administrators not considering the real context, dealing with people of flesh and blood and soul.

The Norwegian researcher Trygve Lie stresses in his definition of integration that 'Integration from a special education view, can be understood as a process of interaction, where participants with different backgrounds are acting without fear of showing or losing identity.'

The original meaning of the Latin word 'integer' was: 'intact, whole', what we today express as 'integrity'. The modern meaning is 'making whole'. This distinction opens up for two levels:

- the individual (keeping whole), and
- the social (making whole).

The German psychologist Helmut Reiser and his research team look upon the process of integration as taking place on four levels:

- individual
- interaction
- institution
- society

According to Reiser, the process is characterised as a process by which one comes to an agreement with oneself and/or each other.

So integration can be viewed from many angles. One can emphasise the individual and his/her needs, the important social context and interaction. One can regard it as a moral or merely administrative matter seen from the angle of the society. But maybe one should acknowledge that as an educator with focus on development processes and using tools of a teacher—communication, stimulation and social interaction—one cannot disregard any angle or level when working for integration.

For the situation in Denmark, with its highly decentralised educational system, one has to add a further level to Reiser's—the level of the local community. I also suggest teacher training as a level.

Thus to talk about, to analyse and evaluate, to promote and to work for and with integration, entails six levels:

1. Level of individuals: The basis of the subsequent levels.
2. Level of interaction: The factual basis for all the processes of integration.
3. Level of institution: The level at which the process is initiated, carried out and recorded. It is the primary administrative basis.
4. Level of society.
5. Level of teaching and teacher training: A prerequisite for the actual process taking place.
6. Level of local community: The level where policy and financial matters are decided.

Towards Inclusive Education

The shift in paradigm from integration to inclusion, which has happened in the English-speaking part of the world, is partly a matter of pointing out that the basis of the discussion on providing for students with disabilities and therefore special needs, should not be from the position of segregation. The word integration implies that there has been first a segregation, while the concept of inclusion starts with the students and their needs. The Swedish researcher Ingemar Emanuelsson suggests that the concept of inclusion focuses on how collective competencies can be developed with the aim of *also* encompassing that part of the multitude and diversity that is regarded negative. Instead of talking of a child as integrated, the concept of inclusion rather talks about the challenges that lie in keeping a group together, which implies a struggle with the processes of segregation.

Demands for Teacher Education

For the enormous task of achieving an inclusive school there is an obvious demand for well educated teachers in special education. This education should take account of:

- Organisation of the teaching-learning situation: To teach in an inclusive class demands a new role for the teacher. The teacher must be able to act as a part of a team, which is mutually responsible for the unified group of students.
- Development of a comprehensive learning approach: The conflicts that may arise between the different students and the diverse demands on facilities, which were 'solved' in the fragmentary integration, will now have to be solved within the classroom. The challenge is to make diverse and different students work and develop together.
- Development of social strategies.
- Holistic view of inclusion\integration: The teacher must secure a co-ordinated collaboration between school, home and leisure time activities. It is important to include the resources of the parents in the actual planning of both teaching-learning activities and social activities.

19

Integrative Education in Israel

Rachel Golan

Israel is a small country with 5.5 million people, which includes 1.2 million pupils from different ethnic, religious, cultural and social backgrounds. In our educational system, about 80 per cent are in the Hebrew-Jewish sector, another 14 per cent in the Arab-Muslim sector, 3 per cent in the Beduin-Muslim sector and about 2 per cent in the Druze sector. In fact integration in Israel is a very important issue.

The Israeli educational system is based on the Jewish philosophy which has placed emphasis on education and study as lifelong obligations. Our educational system has four levels: preschool (5–6 years), primary school (6–12), low secondary school (12–15) and high school (15–18).

The legal base of education in Israel rests on the following laws:

1. Compulsory educational law (1949)—means that education is provided free of charge to all children between 5 and 15 years. Parents must send their children to school, otherwise they are sent to jail.

2. State education law (1953)—means that the state provides a six-day school week and determines the content and procedures of state education. The curriculum has to be approved by the Minister of Education and Culture.

3. School inspection law (1968)—regulates the condition under which schools that are not a part of the state educational system may be opened and operate.

4. Special education law (1988)—provides education for individuals between the ages 3 to 21 whose capacity and adaptive behaviour are limited and who are in need of special education (in process of implementation).

When we say integration, we talk about society. We think about a group of people who are included and others who are excluded whom we want to integrate into the mainstream.

The questions I will deal with are:

1. What is the social role of exceptional people?
2. Is there any reason for society to integrate excluded people?
3. What does integration mean in the Israeli education system?

In order to answer the first question we have to look at educational integration as a special example of a mainstream sociological process. Emile Durkheim, one of the most important sociologists of the twentieth century, wrote that each society excludes people because they play a very important social role. In fact, they mark the margins of society itself and by that help to define it. At a time of change, society defines new margins.

Israeli society is always changing, so our educational system has to do the same. Our educational system has two main subsystems—the regular and the special one. Teacher colleges have two faculties, one for regular teaching and the other for special education. Over the years we discuss again and again who belongs to the regular subsystem and what are the problems which really need special education. Each time we work on the margin we redefine our society.

To answer the second question, whether there is any reason for society to integrate exceptional people, I would like to tell you a story about a girl called Galit. In the year 1975 I got a new group of 12 special education children between ages 8–10 to teach. Galit suffered from cerebral palsy and was the most disabled pupil in my class. She was tiny, walked with a limp and spoke in an unintelligible way. My class was located in a regular school, so Galit had to communicate with her local neighbours. After two years all my pupils were integrated in the regular system including Galit. She made it because she worked hard and I worked with the regular teacher on an individual programme which enabled Galit to stay in her class.

One day Galit got angry about something in class and stood in front of her classmates to tell her problem. When the regular teacher told me about it, I asked her anxiously about the other children's reaction because I knew that it was really difficult to understand her even when she was calm. The teacher's answer gave me one of the most important insights about the real meaning of integration for society. She told me that the children sat in silence for 20 minutes listening to Galit's articulated spoken story, no smiling, no laughing, only admiration in their eyes. When she finished they all cheered her, saying that she gave them an example of how a strong personality can challenge difficulties in life.

Galit taught me that integration gives a chance not only to the disabled student to be part of society, but even more so to the others who learn from the disabled person to fight and overcome challenges.

To answer the third question I will present three organisational models which have been developed in our educational system in order to give the right of equal educational opportunity for many exceptional children in our society. At the time of Galit's story we spoke about integration of pupils. Today we speak about organisational settings which enable teamwork between two or more professionals working with the same child.

As I have already mentioned, in Israel we have two educational subsystems: the regular and the special one.

Integration means organisational developments of teamwork between professionals from the two subsystems at different levels of educational organisation.

There are different organisational models of integrative teamwork which were developed in our regular schools at management level, class level and even city-community level:

1. Special class in regular school
    The teacher of this class is specialised in special education, the curriculum is individualised for each child, but the class is a part of the regular school. Integration is developed by each school, and the children meet and play with their regular schoolmates. My story about Galit is connected with this type. There are two possibilities for integration:
    (a) Individual integration—means special curriculum for one or more pupils from this class. Exceptional children join the regular class during regular subject teaching. Teamwork between the teachers is needed to create continuity between the regular and special teaching.

(b) Group integration—school team works out a special integrative programme for one regular class which is at the same age level as the special class. It is curriculum based, and run by both teachers. The aim of this programme is mainly to achieve social communication and activity.

When I taught the first experimental class in Naharia in the 1970s, it included children with learning disabilities. Today, after almost 20 years, these settings include children who suffer from severe hearing impairment, severe learning disability including cerebral palsy, autistic children and mentally retarded children.

2. Integrated regular class

Mildly handicapped children can learn in regular class if they get support. In order to give the opportunity to these children a model of integrative class was developed by a former head of our special education department.

These classes are built in a ratio of three regular students to one mildly handicapped child. It is a regular class in all senses, but has two teachers: one from the regular subsystem and the other from the special one. Teachers develop a co-teaching pattern of work and both take responsibility for all the pupils of the class.

This organisational model was introduced about 15 years ago in a town called Hertzlia, and today it is well known and established all over Israel. It is relevant to various needs and we find that all parents ask for this model for their children. Regular classes in Israel have 40 children, so that parents of non-handicapped children are happy that their child can get support from two teachers instead of one, and for handicapped children it is a real opportunity to be integrated.

Both these models define two populations—the regular and the special. The third model will show how our educational system helps children with special needs within the regular subsystem. We call this:

3. Community Support Centre

Over 30 years we adapted and developed the American idea of a resource room, where a special education teacher works out an individual educational programme (IEP) for children with special needs in the regular system. This can be a blind child, sight impaired, hearing impaired, physically handicapped, dyslexic or other learning disabled, but it can be also for a child who has been absent for a long time due to illness. In this way the boundary between regular and special needs children becomes blurred, and receiving special help is less of a stigma.

It sounds good but this model created a new problem in our educational system. From a real desire to do good we tended to overdiagnose problems in children. Realising that we have an increasing number of exceptional children, we are trying to correct this imbalance.

In the process of implementing the Special Education Law of 1988—which we have not been able to start doing till recently for lack of funds—the Department of Special Education worked out a national programme which demands fundamental reorganisation. National special education resources will be given according to main budgets: one for children who learn within the regular subsystem of special education, and the other for exceptional children who learn within the regular subsystem.

For exceptional children who are integrated into the regular subsystem, each community gets a fixed 'integration budget' according to the total number of pupils between 5 and 16 and each school gets its proportional share.

The system functions on three levels: community, school and class. Integrative teamwork is developed among different professionals on each level:

(i)   Community level: A Community Support Committee is created and there is a new organisation called Community Support Centre. This centre includes different special education experts—teachers, therapists, etc.—and they are called by schools to advise and work with the child and his/her teacher.

(ii) School level: Each school gets its integrative budget according to its total number of pupils. In this way schools are not allowed to demand extra budget and its regular education team is responsible for all children. The school's interdisciplinary committee with the headteacher as chairman is supposed to work out an individual support programme for children with special needs. School budgets can be used only by asking for teachers and other experts from the Community Support Centre.

(iii) Class level: Co-teaching is the basic work model in the class. Individual education programmes are worked out by an integrative team which includes the regular teacher and the expert from the Community Support Centre.

The Israeli education system is working on a new margin between the regular and the special subsystems and its practical meaning in the development of an integrative philosophy in our society.

20

Mind versus Body: Educational Bias and its Effect in the Cerebral Palsied

Margaret Yekutiel

Physical education is likely to be one of the last areas to consider integration or mainstreaming of disabled children. This is not because it is not amenable to integration—far from it—but because it is given a very low priority in most educational systems: in Israel, for instance, it receives 5 per cent of school hours and less than 1 per cent of the government budget for education.

There is a certain logic in spending so little time and money on the body and so much on the mind, because it is by brain rather than brawn that Man has achieved a dominant position on earth, and success in the modern world owes little to one's physique. But there is a price to pay for this neglect.

This bias is even more marked in education for the physically disabled, notably for the cerebral palsied who often have no physical education at all in their curriculum. This is perhaps because the disabled child is judged to need every available school hour for classroom study if she/he is to reach the academic achievements of able-bodied peers. Another possible reason is that time is allotted for special physiotherapy, occupational or speech therapy, and this may be considered to make up for the lack of physical education. This, as we shall see, is a wrong perception, because the child in special therapy is in general sedentary and often even quite passive.

Until modern times, schoolchildren had ample physical exercise outside the school grounds. They walked to and from school, they played on the streets and in the fields, and the vast majority took some part in the daily work of their parents, family and community. There was no need for the school to teach them to run, jump and climb. Though open spaces for play have shrunk through massive urbanisation and the ubiquitous automobile, the able-bodied child can still exercise out of school through play. However, the time-honoured physical type of play is beginning to be replaced by watching TV and playing computer games, and to this has been linked the decline in physical fitness found in a number of recent surveys of the health of children and adolescents in many Western countries. One can also assume a connection with the startling rise in the proportion of children with dyslexia and related problems.

For cerebral palsied children, the option of play and physical activity outside school scarcely exists. It must be noted too that the more these children are aided by increasingly automated wheelchairs, as well as by helping hands, the less physical challenges will they have and the less need for physical exertion.

Physical inactivity in the cerebral palsied represents a secondary risk factor, compounding the primary damage. Lack of movement and lack of play have profound repercussions on development. We will review Piaget's and other models of the role of movement and experience in the development of perception and present data on some deficits of spatial perception in children with cerebral palsy. In this area, it is often difficult to tell how much is due to lack of movement—'inexperience'—and how much is part of the primary damage. This may be clarified by assessing the effect on spatial perception of the programme of 'Creative movement' which we hope to introduce in the NCCP.

At the other end of the spectrum and less controversial is the severe underdevelopment of respiratory function found in many studies of children with cerebral palsy. The pioneers in this field were Lundberg from Stockholm and Berg from Goteborg, both in Sweden. These and later studies, including a preliminary survey in NCCP in Bombay, found the vital capacity and other measures of respiratory function bring a heightened risk of pneumonia, even of early death, associated with underdeveloped respiratory function. Apart from this, it means a state of low reserve, or decreased energy available for physical activity, to which one must add that a child with cerebral palsy needs much more energy for walking and other activities than an able-bodied child. Here, then, we see a vicious circle: the child with low vital capacity not making the effort to move and thereby exacerbating the condition. Cerebral palsied children tend to become increasingly less active as they grow up. Margalit from Tel-Aviv University, in a recent survey of leisure activities of the cerebral palsied, wrote, 'The children seemed to suffer from boredom and tended to develop a passive lifestyle.'

Until fairly recently, educators and therapists and also parents of cerebral palsied children were afraid that physical activity would increase spasticity and decrease flexibility. This was part of a poor understanding of the subject of spasticity (but it was unfortunately borne out by observations made at the first European Spastics Games, held in London in 1972: these were highly competitive and poorly adapted to the special problems of cerebral palsy). Since then, many studies have shown the great value of adaptive physical activity for the cerebral palsied. These have mainly stressed respiratory function, but an ongoing study of cerebral palsy children exercising regularly at the Wingate Institute in Israel is also monitoring gross motor development, perceptual functions and many aspects of self-image.

21

Bishopwood Story

Mark Vaughan

Bishopwood is a school with nearly 50 pupils but no building. It caters to children with severe learning difficulties aged 2–16 and it gives them a good educational and social experience. This they do through inclusive education. Bishopwood used to be a full-fledged separate special school, but now all the pupils are in mainstream schools and participate actively in the life of those schools.

This chapter gives a brief outline of this inclusion story and concerns children and young people with profound and severe learning difficulties, some with added physical disabilities.

Technically, the 50 disabled children are still on the roll of Bishopwood School which exists in name, at least for the time being. It has its own budget, has its own staff and school governors, but it has given up the building. Instead, it has a base for its pupils in three local ordinary schools.

If you visited these ordinary schools in Oxfordshire, England today, where all 50 children are now educated, it would be difficult to pick them all out. They share many of the same lessons, have the same school uniform, eat the same meals, join the same clubs, are in the same playground at break time, and so on.

As a separate special school, Bishopwood was in splendid, purpose-built accommodation and grounds, with all the equipment, resources, staff, shiny clean floors and therapy pool you could wish for. But, for the headteacher and the staff, that was not enough.

The things that were missing were relationships. Relationships with non-disabled children of their same age. So 16 years ago, in 1981, a first group of infant-aged children (5–7 years) with severe learning difficulties moved into a classroom of their own at the nearby Sonning Common Primary School.

It was the beginning of a 10-year process that was to see the gradual emptying of this special school and the transfer of all the pupils, the teaching and non-teaching staff, equipment and resources, to ordinary nursery, primary and comprehensive (or secondary) schools. Slowly, class by class the children and staff moved across to the appropriate-aged ordinary schools.

The actual classroom education of Bishopwood pupils begins in the base room and—depending on a variety of factors—leads to a gradual increase in the pupil's placement in the regular classrooms, in different parts of the ordinary schools. The amount of time spent in each classroom varies according to each child.

After about five years of good progress, when half of the special school population had moved, there was a hiatus while everyone considered what to do with the remaining 50 per cent of the Bishopwood children who had more complex disabilities and difficulties. It did not take long to decide to work towards the transfer of 100 per cent of pupils, and this was completed by 1990.

In the words of the headteacher: 'The facilities available to us now at all the mainstream sites are as good as those left behind in the purpose-built special school, and, in the case of the comprehensive school, much better.' If there is any difficulty with the mainstream peer group, say the teachers, it is that the non-disabled children want to help too much!

There is a radical philosophy behind this change in the education of a group of children and young people with severe learning difficulties, some of whom also have additional complicating disabilities such as sensory impairment or who are wheelchair users.

It is pioneering work, and it proves that something that was considered impossible—and is still considered impossible by many people in the UK—has become a very successful and effective way of giving a full educational and social experience to these disabled pupils.

The transition from the enormous investments in tailor-made, expensive, segregated institutions to the position today has been a very well managed and smooth changeover. It has been carefully thought through and has been beneficial to all, both disabled and non-disabled pupils alike.

Ten years ago a study was done to gauge the feelings of parents of non-disabled pupils towards the plans for inclusion, before it took place, and then again, after it had happened. Prior to the changes, the majority of parents showed strong opposition and anxiety; after the inclusion of disabled pupils was established, that opposition switched to 93 per cent support! The parents of mainstream pupils actively wanted the Bishopwood pupils in ordinary schools.

At CSIE we called the 1992 report we published about Bishopwood 'Good Practice Transferred' because that is precisely what happened. The Bishopwood Special School Staff were very clear about their philosophical conviction supporting the inclusion of their children in the mainstream, and they proved it was possible to transfer the good practice and, in so doing, provide an even better education for their pupils.

The head and teaching staff believe that Bishopwood, and other special schools like them, were originally created to house a population of children whose disability or learning difficulty, it was felt, prevented them from receiving education in ordinary schools.

CSIE puts it another way—special schools exist because of the failings of ordinary schools. And special schools will continue to exist if mainstream schools do not adapt and change—that is, re-structure—in order to include those traditionally excluded from the ordinary school experience.

This restructuring and re-evaluation of 'What is school for?' is a vital aspect of inclusion, as has been shown by the Bishopwood story.

The Bishopwood teaching staff themselves quoted this part of the 1975 United Nations Declaration of the Rights of Disabled People to support their proposals for change:

> 'Whatever the origin, nature and seriousness of their handicaps and disabilities, disabled people have the same fundamental rights as their fellow citizens of the same age, which implies first and foremost the right to a decent life as normal and as full as possible.'

According to the Bishopwood teachers, those rights should apply to all pupils with special educational needs, including those with severe learning problems.

Some of the advantages of the Bishopwood inclusion model are:

- disabled pupils' self-esteem, motivation and confidence have grown;
- use of language and behaviour have improved;

- the mainstream schools offer a wider range of educational and social experiences than that possible at special schools;
- disabled pupils come to terms with their limitations supported by friends of similar ability;
- Bishopwood staff have the opportunity to widen their teaching experience; and
- a genuine continuum of provision is provided from nursery to further education.

While the achievements of Bishopwood School are considerable, I do have some reservations about the status of the special school being maintained. The question has to be asked: Why not go the whole way and dismantle the infrastructure of Bishopwood and simply let the children belong to the local ordinary school?

The Bishopwood staff say they would not have been able to achieve what they have done so far if they had given up the legal and financial status of being a special school, and that it is too risky for their children to move fully onto the roll of the partner schools at present.

They point out that Oxfordshire education authority, a lot of schools and people generally, are in two minds about the importance of inclusive education. This makes them reluctant to 'hand over' their pupils and relinquish control, yet. It is also true that the present system of financing special education in England favours the current Bishopwood model: they get extra resources in terms of staffing, capitation, etc., because they are legally a special school and those funds are targeted towards these children.

Equalisation of Opportunity: What Does it Mean?

Malini Chib

Introduction

I have a speech impediment. My speech is monotonous, and when I utter some words, my speech comes out in an infantile manner and inarticulate. The sound that comes out from my throat frustrates me. When I listen to my own voice on a tape recorder or an answer phone, I want to run a mile as I can't bear the sound of my own voice. I don't know how my family and friends put up with it. Well, it takes people a long time to understand me, so I use a voice synthesizer to talk, but they do eventually! If they can't understand me the first time, I usually spell it out until they have got it. It's an endless effort between the listener and me, but we finally get there. Once people get to understand my speech, I grab the rare opportunity, and you will find I cannot stop talking!

Definition

Let me begin with some definitions of the word Spastic.

The term 'spastic' in the Webster dictionary is defined as 'drawing or pulling.... 1. Characterized by, affected with, or produced by spasm 2. Afflicted with or involving spastic paralysis. This is a medical definition saying very little about me as a person, how I think and feel.

Then I looked at the word 'enclosure'. Some terms came up immediately: cage, jail and restrict. For the word 'impediment' two words came up—'hindrance' and 'obstacle'. For the word 'integration' some interesting words are desegregate, mix, unite and combine. For the word 'include', involve, embrace and encompass—words are so important.

Chris Davis who is a pàrt-time teacher, writer and broadcaster has cerebral palsy. Chris is a special school survivor and has attended three segregated schools. He writes about how disability is no longer internally based on a set of physical or mental restrictions; instead, disability has an external source in social attitudes, behaviour and environmental barriers (Davis, 1993). If the world in which disabled people live was not designed on the assumption that it is mainly for those who can walk and talk etc., disabled people would be free and equal. Precisely because the world is designed this way, it creates a society in which disabled people do not fit the norm. He goes on to say that by the new way of thinking—the social model of disability—we disabled people are accepted as we are; we do not want to deny our difference. The old definition had the value judgements inherent in the medical model of disability. The social definition, instead of looking inwards and trying to force change on us in order to be assimilated into mainstream society, says that mainstream society has itself to change to become less disabling for people like us.

My Background

Let me tell you a bit about my educational background. I am a product of special schools, having spent 16 years of my life in them. First, in Cheyne Walk in London, then in the Centre for Special Education, in Bombay, for about eight years. At that time, it was the need of the hour to establish a special school, as there were no special schools for children like us in India.

The environment both in India and the UK was extremely caring and protective. Socially, all my classmates used to live at the other end of the city. There was no peer interaction after school hours. I was not able to do the ordinary things like gossiping on the telephone, or going out for a drink or a meal, or shopping.

When I went to a regular school (Xaviers), I noticed the gap acutely between the able-bodied and the disabled. I was only the second person who was disabled—Farhan my classmate was the other. The first few days we stood out like sore thumbs as we sat on the front bench. When we both said our names, it sounded as if we were from outer space. I suffered a great deal from acute social isolation. My friends were few and superficial—Hi and Bye types. Socially, I was inept and my conversation skills were extremely limited. Rather than being with one group of people, I would roam about on my own, but I soon found that I was being more and more excluded from the social scene, which you will agree is a major and vital part of college life.

My self esteem took a nose-dive. I began questioning myself—Did I have anything to contribute? Did they like me only because of my disability? No one really wanted to get to know me deeply. It was a painful process which I have not yet been able to overcome.

Strangely, again, when I was in Oxford, doing a diploma in publishing, I was the first student with special needs that my lecturers had encountered. Initially, they were hesitant. It took them a while to get used to my out of the ordinary ways, however, they were most helpful. They were most apologetic about the fact that the department was up one flight of stairs, so whenever I wanted a quick word they would come down. They were most attentive to my needs. By the end of the course they could understand my speech 50 per cent. For the examination, I was told that all the publishing students were having a mock interview, for a job in a publishing house, and it would count as 30 per cent of a paper. Secretly I was looking forward to it as I had never experienced a viva before. But as the days progressed, I heard rumours from past students that the two professors were very tough. The days passed too quickly. Before I knew it the day had arrived. I was so nervous as I was convinced that I did not know very much. I took a friend who understood my speech extremely well. I walked in. My two professors sat before the table looking rather formal. Question after question was fired at me. I had to speak articulately. There was no beating around the bush. Both of my professors grilled me and saw to it that every ounce of knowledge was questioned and regurgitated. I did well and passed. I had come full circle in one year. A year ago, my professors did not know anything about me as a student with special needs, but after dealing with me for the year, they no longer thought I had problems; in fact, they treated me so equally at times it was difficult!

Attitudes

Attitudes matter a great deal. Most people still look at me as a child, although I am a 30-year-old woman. Even today, many who do not know me or may not have met a disabled person before in their life will automatically address the person who I am with, about me, in front of me, but never to me. And then afterwards they will ask, 'Does she understand?' Or 'She went to Oxford? How nice! Can she hear?' And the conversation will proceed no further! I have to keep on proving myself to everybody that I am intelligent and I can understand. Sometimes it is irritating and I want to scream, but instead it is a silent cry.

What about my needs as a woman? What about life, marriage, sex? Professionals and rehabilitation workers usually brush off the topic with 'It doesn't concern you, dear, you are still a child. Why should you worry?' They get embarrassed so they evade certain topics. Deep down they are convinced that no one will marry me.

Personal relationships have been the least successful part of my life. Lack of opportunity and lack of experience have meant social isolation which is difficult to constantly live with. This has been quite complete with the environmental barriers.

The Impact of Segregation

The impact of being segregated is largely inexplicable. The older I get, the more excluded I feel. Maybe because when I was young I had to keep proving to others that I was intelligent and that I could contribute to society in whatever minute way.

As I grow older, I feel the stares of the common man pierce through my body like a knife. For me to feel included by society, I need an electric wheelchair and a voice synthesizer. I am a different person if I have them with me. They give me confidence that I can do anything I want.

However trivial it may sound, it boosts my confidence if I am able to go out shopping or even for a walk. The pleasure of roaming the streets and having the freedom and being anonymous...the feeling that you are different lessens considerably. I thought I had overcome the stares and the banal questions about me. The way people talk in front of me, about me, should not affect me but sometimes it still does, now more than ever, or the way people feel embarrassed and do not talk to me at parties.

I think two of the most important things for integration are people's attitudes and barriers in the environment. I feel nobody is perfect, that life is imperfect and the main question seems to be whether the so-called normal or able-bodied are able to accept disability or accept me as someone different.

In a country where there are no ramps in shops, colleges or offices, there are no disabled toilets, the pavements are inaccessible, where everything is geared for the normal, where there are social, psychological, emotional and mental blocks against the disabled, it makes me wonder are we really citizens of India? Are we free?

Reference

Davis, C. (1993) *Life time—A Mutual Biography of Disabled People. Understanding Disabled in Educational Technology (UDET).* Compiled by Chris Davis.

Annexure

A. Title of the Seminar:
   Integrated Education for Chidren with Special Needs—A Matter of Social Justice and Human Rights

B. Aim of the Seminar:
   1. Focus on problems impeding equalisation of opportunity and mainstreaming children with special needs in India.
   2. Focus on international perspectives in mainstreaming as well as mainstreaming in some developing countries.
   3. Develop policy strategy in India.

C. Target Audience:
   1. People with special needs;
   2. Parents of people with special needs and their siblings;
   3. Principals, professionals and senior staff of normal schools;
   4. Principals, professionals and senior staff of special schools;
   5. Principals, professionals and senior staff of integrated schools;
   6. DPEP policy makers;
   7. Education policy makers;
   8. Disabled activists;
   9. Media;
   10. Government.

D. Venue and Dates for the Seminar:
   Mumbai: 30 and 31 January and 1 February 1997. National Centre for Cerebral Palsy, Research and Training Auditorium.
   New Delhi: 7 and 8 February 1997. India International Centre, Conference Hall.
   Jaipur: 12 February 1997. Indian Institute of Health Management Research.

E. Collaborators:

The Spastics Society of India

Ministry of Human Resource Development, New Delhi

NCERT, National Council for Education Research and Training, New Delhi

NIEPA, National Institute for Education Planning & Administration, New Delhi

NCTE, National Council for Teacher Education, New Delhi

CSIE, Centre for Studies in Inclusive Education, UK

Ministry of State for Education, Mumbai

DISHA, Jaipur

Institute of Health, Management Research, Jaipur

The Spastics Society of Northern India, New Delhi

The Spastics Society of India, Chennai

F. Themes and Sub-themes:

I. Plenary Session I

National and International Perspectives:

1. Developing Countries
2. Developed Countries

Sub Themes:

1. Historical
2. Legislation and Policy Options for Children with Special Needs
3. Codes of Practice
4. Alternative Paradigms of Integration

II. Plenary Session II

Practicalities of Integration: A National and International Exchange:

1. Locational and Environmental
2. Curriculum Modification
3. Early Years
4. Identification/Assessment
5. Resource Support
6. Teacher Training
7. Linkages, Monitoring, Evaluation
8. Current Research Trends

G. Co-Chairperson:

Mr P.R. Dasgupta, Secretary, Ministry of Education, Human Resources Development, Government of India, New Delhi and Dr Mithu Alur, Founder Chairperson, The Spastics Society of India.

Glossary

Anganwadi: Centres for delivery of package of services under ICDS in a village/ urban slum. Literally a courtyard playgroup for children in the age group 0–6 run by anganwadi workers usually selected from the local village or local slum area.

BMC: The Brihanmumbai Municipal Corporation, the local authority in Bombay to provide education, health, transport and other civic amenities like water, electricity and roads.

NDMC: New Delhi Municipal Corporation.

Balwadis: A child day-care nursery for age group of 3–6.

Bustees/Jhopadpattis: Other terms to describe slum-like conditions and people living not in proper concrete housing but in huts or shacks in a shanty town spread.

Chawls: Indian term for a slum in the cities. A common characteristics of all slums is substandard housing, lack of basic amenities such as water, sewage facilities.

Central government: Refers to highest levels of government under India's federal system that comprises of 29 states and union territories.

Mahila mandals: women's cooperatives.

State government: Refers to the government of a particular state in India.

About the Editors and Contributors

Seamus Hegarty is Director of the National Foundation for Educational Research in England and Wales. He is also Editor of *Educational Research* and Founder Editor of the *European Journal of Special Needs Education* besides serving on the editorial board of five other special needs journals. Author of various reports and position papers for UNESCO, Dr Hegarty has had an extensive involvement with that organisation in promoting inclusive education. He also has a long track record of research and activity in special needs education, and has published numerous books and papers on the subject.

Mithu Alur is an educationist, a social reformer and an academic activist. Founder Chairperson of The Spastics Society of India and a recipient of the Padamshri (1989), she has published numerous articles and research studies on children with special needs. At that state-level, she has been involved with various community-based projects involving state municipal authorities, NGOs, the private sector and international agencies. Dr Alur has also set up a postgraduate diploma course for teacher training and has been involved in the training of teachers and specialists such as therapists, social workers, doctors and community workers.

Anupam Ahuja is an education researcher from the NCERT, and has been involved with integration aspects for a long time. She has published articles on the subject in many symposia and conferences. She has worked in different parts of the world and has trained teachers to meet the needs of children with special needs. Presently, she is involved in a Ph.D. programme.

Father P.T. Augustine is Principal of St. Xavier's Senior Secondary School in Jaipur. His research interests are new ideas and approaches of experimentation with special focus on equal opportunities for various sections of society, especially children with special educational needs.

Ruma Banerjee is one of the directors of Seva-in-Action, a leading voluntary organisation in Bangalore. She has developed innovative models of community-based rehabilitation and represented the organisation in several conferences and seminars in India and abroad.

Malini Chib is a freelance writer activist and advocate of equal opportunities and full participation for the disabled. She is also one of the Trustees of the Spastics Society of India. She has travelled extensively in India and abroad and has published several articles. She has presented papers in international and national conferences. A graduate in History Honours from Bombay University, Malini Chib has an advanced diploma in Publishing from Brookes University, Oxford. She is presently doing her masters in Women's Studies at the Institute of Education, University of London.

P.R. Dasgupta is Secretary of the Ministry of Education and Human Resources Development of the Government of India. Mr Dasgupta is keenly interested in the cause of the disabled and believes in the equalisation of opportunities. He has participated and presented papers on universalisation of primary education at various conferences. He is also takes active interest in planning innovative techniques for integrated education.

Rachel Golan has done an M.A. in Sociology of Organisations from the University of Bar-Hab and a B.A. in Education and Sociology from the University of Har, Haifa. In the year 1995, she worked as an organisation counsellor at the national level for the implementation of Special Education Law as well as in the Special Education Department. She was actively working as an organisational supervisor of Different Integrative Educational Projects Special Education Departments in the Primary Education Department and Teacher Education Department in 1994–95. She is also a member of the Curriculum Development Team within the Mofel Institute in the Teacher Education Department. She is a writer and nation wide supervisor of implementation of the 'Integration of Special Education Class into Regular Primary Schools Programme' in 1992–94. She was school counsellor in a regular primary school and district supervisor in special education in 1989–92.

Peter Gam Henriksen is an educational planner by profession. He has specialised in educational programmes, evaluation, institutional development, staff development and educational planning. He was Director at the Greenland Teacher's Training College in 1979–80. He was the European Commission representative in India in 1995 for the Evaluation of the Monitoring and Evaluation Strategy of the District Primary Education Programme (DPEP), New Delhi.

N.K. Jangira is former director of the National Centre for Special Education, Training and Research. Professor Jangira is presently with the World Bank. A senior education researcher and teacher educator in India, Professor Jangira has published several research articles in international and national journals. He is well known for his contributions to the field of teacher training and education in African countries.

Deepak Kalra has done her M.Sc. in Child Development from M.S. University in Baroda. She has worked for several years as a teacher educator and researcher. She has put in many years of work at the Spastics Society of India. At present, she is the principal of Disha, a school for children with multiple disabilities in Jaipur. She has presented papers in national and international conferences and has lectured on the Spastics Society's postgraduate teacher training courses.

Pearl Kavoori has over 50 years of experience as a teacher, administrator and head of a mainstream school. She is very keen on inclusion issues and a rights approach to disability. She is one of the trustees of Disha, a special school for children with disabilities.

Amena Latif is vice-principal of the Centre for Special Education, Bandra. Her entire education has been in integrated schools. Having experienced the advantages, barrier and hard work of her mother, she is now an advocate of inclusion. She has over 15 years of experience in formal and non-formal education of children with special needs, pre-vocational training, parent training, and assisting the postgraduate teacher training course.

M.N.G. Mani is principal of Ramakrishna Mission College of Education in Coimbatur. Mr Mani is an education planner and researcher. He is keenly interested in integrated education of disabled and has done a great deal of work in the area of cost-effective approaches of integrated education for the disabled.

Sudesh Mukhopadhyay is currently Director, State Council for Education, Research and Training (SCERT), New Delhi. She has researched extensively in the field of education from the NCERT. In her supervisory capacity she is involved in the process of curriculum planning for achieving the goal of Universalisation of Primary Education by 2000 AD.

Madhuri Pai has done her B.Sc. from Pune University in 1974 and her M.Sc from I.I.T., Bombay in 1976. She completed her Ph.D. in Physics in 1980. She has taught undergraduate students for four years in Bombay University and postgraduate students for three years in Bombay University and Pune University. Currently, she is the Director of Training at the Spastics Society of India, National Centre for Cerebral Palsy, Bandra.

Reena Sen is a psychologist by training and has done her Ph.D. from the Institute of Education, London University. She has many years of experience working with children with special needs. Currently she is Director of Education at the Spastics Society of Eastern India, Institute of Cerebral Palsy, Calcutta.

Usha Singh is principal of a well known school in Jaipur. She has several years of experience with disabled children with a special view to mainstreaming them.

Karl-Gustaf Stukat is a professor of general and special education. He is engaged in a research project on special education and compensatory education sponsored by UNESCO, OECD and Council of Europe. He was a member of several national committees for educational research in Sweden, and is a member of the editorial board of the *European Journal of Special Needs Education*. He has a number of publications to his credit. He is the author of *Integration of Pupils with Motor Disabilities*, a book on integration (Malmo, 1996). At present he is involved in a research project on the cognitive and learning development of motor disabled children in an inclusive educational setting.

Mark Vaughan is an educationist from UK. He is founder and co-director of the Centre for Studies in Inclusive Education. He worked as a journalist for many years and was also the editor of the education supplement of *The Times*, London. Mr Vaughan has also worked at the advisory centre for education in London. He is an advocate of inclusive education and has published several articles on the subject.

Margaret Yekutiel was born and educated in England, did a B.A. in Biology and a Ph.D. in Medical Science from Oxford in 1953. She did her postgraduate studies at Harvard and then immigrated to Israel and worked as a medical statistician. In 1967, almost in midlife, she switched to Physiotherapy which she studied in Mexico. She teaches and is also involved in clinical research of strokes, Parkinson's and CP. Recently retired from the University of Ben-Gurion, Beer-Sheva, Dr Yekutiel has been associated with the Spastics Society of India for several years.

Index